LLEWELLYN'S
2015

Witches'
Spell-A-Day
Almanac

Holidays & Lore
Spells, Rituals & Meditations

Copyright 2014 Llewellyn Worldwide Ltd.
Cover Design: Lisa Novak
Editing: Andrea Neff

Background photo: © PhotoDisc
Interior Art: © 2011, Steven McAfee
pp. 13, 33, 53, 73, 93, 111, 131, 151, 171, 191, 213, 233
Spell icons throughout: © 2011 Sherrie Thai

You can order Llewellyn books and annuals from *New Worlds*,
Llewellyn's catalog. To request a free copy of the catalog, call toll-free
1-877-NEW WRLD or visit our website at www.llewellyn.com.

ISBN: 978-0-7387-2692-2
Llewellyn is a registered trademark of Llewellyn Worldwide Ltd.
2143 Wooddale Drive
Woodbury, MN 55125

Printed in the United States of America

Contents

About the Authors

Barbara Ardinger, PhD (www.barbaraardinger.com and www.facebook
.com/barbara.ardinger), is the author of *Secret Lives*, a novel about crones
and other magical folks, and *Pagan Every Day*, a unique daybook of daily
meditations. Her other books include *Goddess Meditations* (the first-ever
book of meditations focusing on goddesses), *Finding New Goddesses* (a
parody of goddess encyclopedias), and an earlier novel, *Quicksilver Moon*
(which is realistic… except for the vampire). Her monthly blogs appear
on her website and on *Feminism and Religion*, feminismandreligion.com,
where she is one of three regular Pagan contributors. Barbara lives in
Long Beach, California, with her two rescued Maine coon cats.

Elizabeth Barrette has been involved with the Pagan community for more
than twenty-four years. She served as Managing Editor of *PanGaia* for
eight years and Dean of Studies at the Grey School of Wizardry for four
years. Her book *Composing Magic: How to Create Magical Spells, Rituals,
Blessings, Chants, and Prayers* explains how to combine writing and spirituality. She lives in central Illinois, where she has done much networking with
Pagans in her area, such as coffeehouse meetings and open sabbats. Visit
her blog, *The Wordsmith's Forge* (http://ysabetwordsmith.livejournal.com),
or her website, *PenUltimate Productions* (http://penultimateproductions.
weebly.com). Her coven site, with extensive Pagan materials, is *Greenhaven
Tradition* (http://greenhaventradition.weebly.com).

Blake Octavian Blair is an eclectic Pagan, ordained minister, shamanic
practitioner, writer, Usui Reiki Master-Teacher, tarot reader, and musical artist. Blake blends various mystical traditions from both the East and
West along with a reverence for the natural world into his own brand of
modern Neo-Paganism and magick. Blake holds a degree in English and
Religion from the University of Florida. He is an avid reader, crafter, and
practicing vegetarian. Blake lives with his beloved husband, an aquarium
full of fish, and an indoor jungle of houseplants. Visit him on the web at
www.blakeoctavianblair.com or write him at blake@blakeoctavianblair.com.

Thuri Calafia is the author of *Dedicant: A Witch's Circle of Fire* and *Initiate:
A Witch's Circle of Water*. She is an ordained minister, a Wiccan High
Priestess, a teacher, and the creator of the Circles system and school.
She lives and is actively involved in the Pagan community in the Pacific
Northwest while attending college and working on her third Circles series
book, *Adept: A Witch's Circle of Earth*.

Raven Digitalis (Missoula, MT) is the author of *Shadow Magick Compendium*, *Planetary Spells & Rituals*, and *Goth Craft*, all published by Llewellyn. He is a Neopagan Priest and cofounder of an Eastern Hellenistic coven and order called *Opus Aima Obscuræ (OAO)*, and is a DJ of Gothic and industrial music. Also trained in Georgian Witchcraft and Buddhist philosophy, Raven has been a Witch since 1999, a Priest since 2003, a Freemason since 2012, and an Empath all his life. Raven holds a degree in anthropology from the University of Montana and is also a professional Tarot reader, small-scale farmer, and animal rights advocate. He has appeared on the cover of *newWitch* magazine and *Spellcraft* magazine, and has been featured on various print, radio, and television media outlets, including MTV News. Visit him at www.raven digitalis.com or www.facebook.com/ravendigitalisauthor.

Emyme, an eclectic solitary, resides in a multi-generation, multi-cat household in Southern New Jersey—concentrating on candle spells, garden spells, and kitchen witchery. In addition to writing poetry and prose about strong women of mythology and fairy tales, Emyme is creating a series of articles on bed & breakfasts from the point of view of the over-fifty-five, single, female, Wiccan traveler. Please send questions or comments to catsmeow24@verizon.net.

Boudica Foster is best known for her professional reviews of books on Paganism and its various paths. Boudica and her husband ran the successful *Wiccan/Pagan Times* website till they retired it recently to pursue other ventures. She also ran the *Zodiac Bistro* website, a repository of articles, commentaries, and reviews by Boudica, for many years till she retired that recently as well. She is a self-published author. Boudica is a staunch supporter of building Pagan community and has worked in covens as well as having a solitary practice. In the past she has presented at many events in the Northeast and Ohio. She still presents occasionally at events and holds public workshops in the Northeast. She runs an online bookstore and reads tarot cards for clients. Boudica lives in Bucks County, Pennsylvania, with her husband of many years and her cats.

Michael Furie (Northern California) is the author of *Spellcasting for Beginners* and *Supermarket Magic*, both published by Llewellyn, and has been a practicing Witch for over eighteen years. He began studying Witchcraft at age twelve and at the age of seventeen officially took the oaths of the Craft. An American Witch, he practices in the Irish tradition and is a priest of the Cailleach. You can find him online at www.michaelfurie.com.

Ember Grant is the author of two books, *Magical Candle Crafting* and *The Book of Crystal Spells*, and she has been writing for the Llewellyn annuals since 2003. Ember is a college English teacher and also enjoys nature photography and gardening. Visit her at embergrant.com.

James Kambos is an artist and writer from Ohio. He enjoys studying folk magic and working with the Tarot.

Estha McNevin (Missoula, MT) is the founding Priestess and oracle of the Eastern Hellenistic magickal temple *Opus Aima Obscuræ (OAO)*. As High Priestess of OAO, she offers over a decade of experience in teaching concise Pagan history, metaphysical skills, ritual practicum, and rural arts. In the greater community she works as a lecturer, baker, writer, organic gardener, and psychic intuitive and is co-owner of the metaphysical business *Twigs & Brews*. In addition to hosting public rituals for the sabbats, Estha organizes spiritual and civil rights publications, public holiday events, and women's divination rituals each Dark Moon. She conducts private spiritual consultations, spirit intermediations, and Tarot readings for the greater Pagan community. Visit her at www.facebook.com/opusaimaobscurae.

Susan Pesznecker is a writer, college English teacher, and hearth Pagan/Druid living in northwestern Oregon. Her magickal roots include Pictish Scot and Eastern European/Native American medicine traditions. Sue holds a master's degree in nonfiction writing and loves to read, stargaze, camp with her wonder poodle, and play in her biodynamic garden. She's co-founder of the Druid Grove of Two Coasts (find the Grove on Facebook) and teaches nature studies and herbalism in the online Grey School. Sue has authored *Crafting Magick with Pen and Ink* (Llewellyn, 2009) and *The Magickal Retreat* (Llewellyn, 2012) and regularly contributes to the Llewellyn annuals. Visit her at www.susanpesznecker.com and www.facebook.com/SusanMoonwriterPesznecker.

Laurel Reufner's mother can verify that she grew up a "wild child" in farming country. Laurel has been earth-centered for around a quarter century and really enjoys writing about whatever topics grab her attention. She has always lived in southeastern Ohio and currently calls Athens County home, where she lives with her wonderful husband and two wild daughters of her own. Find her online at *Laurel Reufner's Lair*, http://laurelreufner .blogspot.com, or on Facebook.

Tess Whitehurst is the author of five books, including *The Magic of Flowers*, *Magical Fashionista*, and *Magical Housekeeping*. She's also a feng shui consultant and intuitive counselor. Visit her online and sign up for her free monthly newsletter at www.tesswhitehurst.com, and find her on Facebook at www.facebook.com/TessWhitehurstAuthor.

When she's not on the road or chasing free-range hens, **Natalie Zaman** is trying to figure out the universe. She is the co-author of the *Graven Images Oracle deck* (Galde Press) and the YA novels *Sirenz* and *Sirenz Back in Fashion* (Flux) and *Blonde Ops* (St. Martin's Press). Her work has appeared in *Llewellyn's Magical Almanac*, *FATE*, *SageWoman*, and *newWitch* magazines, and she currently writes the recurring feature "Wandering Witch" for *Witches & Pagans* magazine. Find Natalie online at http://nataliezaman.com, or at http://broomstix.blogspot.com, a collection of crafts, stories, ritual, and art she curates for Pagan families.

A Note on Magic and Spells

The spells in the *Witches' Spell-A-Day Almanac* evoke everyday magic designed to improve our lives and homes. You needn't be an expert on magic to follow these simple rites and spells; as you will see if you use these spells throughout the year, magic, once mastered, is easy to perform. The only advanced technique required of you is the art of visualization.

Visualization is an act of controlled imagination. If you can call up in your mind a picture of your best friend's face or a flag flapping in the breeze, you can visualize. In magic, visualizations are used to direct and control magical energies. Basically the spellcaster creates a visual image of the spell's desired goal, whether it be perfect health, a safe house, or a protected pet.

Visualization is the basis of all good spells, and as such it is a tool that should be properly used. Visualization must be real in the mind of the spellcaster so it allows him or her to raise, concentrate, and send forth energy to accomplish the spell.

Perhaps when visualizing you'll find that you're doing everything right, but you don't feel anything. This is common, for we haven't been trained to acknowledge—let alone utilize—our magical abilities. Keep practicing, however, for your spells can "take" even if you're not the most experienced natural magician.

You will notice also that many spells in this collection have a some-what "light" tone. They are seemingly fun and frivolous, filled with rhyme and colloquial speech. This is not to diminish the seriousness of the purpose, but rather to create a relaxed atmosphere for the practitio-ner. Lightness of spirit helps focus energy; rhyme and common language help the spellcaster remember the words and train the mind where it is needed. The intent of this magic is indeed very serious at times, and magic is never to be trifled with.

Even when your spells are effective, magic won't usually sparkle before your very eyes. The test of magic's success is time, not immedi-ate eye-popping results. But you can feel magic's energy for yourself by rubbing your palms together briskly for ten seconds, then holding them a few inches apart. Sense the energy passing through them, the warm tin-gle in your palms. This is the power raised and used in magic. It comes from within and is perfectly natural.

Among the features of the *Witches' Spell-A-Day Almanac* are an easy-to-use "book of days" format; new spells specifically tailored for each day of the year (and its particular magical, astrological, and historical energies); and additional tips and lore for various days throughout the year—including color correspondences based on planetary influences, obscure and forgotten holidays and festivals, and an incense of the day to help you waft magical energies from the ether into your space. Moon signs, phases, and voids are also included to help you find the perfect time for your rituals and spells.

Enjoy your days, and have a magical year!

Spell–A–Day Icons

 New Moon

 Meditation, Divination

 Full Moon

 Money, Prosperity

 Abundance

 Protection

 Altar

 Relationship

 Balance

 Success

 Clearing, Cleaning

 Travel, Communication

 Garden

 Air Element

 Grab Bag

 Earth Element

 Health, Healing

 Fire Element

 Home

 Spirit Element

 Heart, Love

 Water Element

Spells at a Glance by Date and Category*

	Health	Protection	Success	Heart, Love	Clearing, Cleaning	Home	Meditation, Divination
Jan.	22, 24	6, 14, 29	3, 18, 26		8, 10, 12		7, 21
Feb.			8	9, 13, 14, 20, 24, 27	16	12, 19, 23	5, 15, 28
March	16	1, 10, 29	22, 31	6	11, 23	3	17, 30
April			19, 29	3, 10	20	1	2, 5, 11, 15, 25
May	6	5, 12, 29		10, 23		15	2, 13, 17, 27, 30
June	15		24	5	4, 23, 25, 27	13	
July	6, 12	5, 27	2, 17, 28		8, 14, 18		4
Aug.	10, 17, 24	7, 30, 31	1, 6, 8, 18, 20		4	16	2, 11, 15
Sept.	5, 18	4, 7	20, 30		11, 19	17	9, 10, 12, 24, 26, 28
Oct.	6, 16, 19, 24	2, 3, 5, 11		26	14, 31		9, 13, 22
Nov.	5, 8, 18	13, 23	1, 19	17	27	14	3, 7, 29, 30
Dec.	1, 4, 6, 15, 19, 28	26, 31		7, 18		8, 22	9, 13, 30

*List is not comprehensive.

2015

Year of Spells

January

Before Julius Caesar hired the astronomer Sosigenes of Alexandria in 46 BCE to reform the calendar, the year began with the spring equinox. But the traditional calendar had gotten out of sync with the seasons. The new Julian calendar remained in effect until it, too, fell out of sync and was reformed in 1582 by Pope Gregory XIII. The Gregorian calendar is today's common calendar, though some religions still use variations of the Julian calendar.

January is named for Janus (Ianus), the two-faced Roman god of the doorway, which is the transition point between the safe indoors and the outside world, where anything might happen. Before Janus came to the city, he was Dianus, an Italian oak god whose consort was the woodland goddess Diana. The Romans weren't alone in believing that this opening needed to be protected. The mezuzah, which holds verses from Deuteronomy, is affixed to doors of Jewish houses. Medieval cathedrals feature elaborate façades around their doorways, and nearly every Pagan is taught to cut a "doorway" into the energy of the circle.

When we do January magic, let's focus on openings, closings, and transitions. What are we closing? What are we opening?

Barbara Ardinger, PhD

January 1

Thursday

2nd ♉

☽ v/c 7:19 am

☽ → ♊ 12:09 pm

Color of the day: Green

Incense of the day: Nutmeg

New Year's Day – Kwanzaa ends

Expand into Abundance

Welcome to the first day of your most expansive, joyful, and luxurious year yet! Today, set the intention to welcome in avalanches of positivity and abundance. Fortify the intention by clearing old receipts and clutter out of your wallet and purse, then dust and sweep your entire home as you chant:

Welcome and merry meet, 2015!
Welcome and merry meet, happiness, joy, wealth, abundance, and luck!

Seal the deal and magnetize your intention by lighting a bright red votive candle and a stick of vanilla, jasmine, or cinnamon incense. Move throughout each room and area with the candle and incense (carefully catching any burning embers with a plate or incense holder) as you visualize very bright golden light filling your heart, home, and life. Finally, place the candle and incense on your altar or in a central location, and allow them to burn all the way down.

Tess Whitehurst

 January 2

Friday

2nd ♊

Color of the day: Rose

Incense of the day: Yarrow

Double Happiness

Numerologically, January 2, 2015, adds up to 2. Think about the energy of this number: duality (the presence of light and dark), balance, and, of course, doubling. To double your happiness in the coming year, write out the numerological formula of the day on a piece of paper:

01/02/2015

$1 + 2 + 2 + 0 + 1 + 5 = 11 =$
$1 + 1 = 2$

Turn the paper over and write this spell, being sure to focus and believe in the words:

Double, double,

No toil,

No trouble.

In the coming year, my joy is double!

Burn the paper to offer it up to the universe—and know you will have a good year! This spell can be performed on any day that adds up to 2.

Natalie Zaman

January 3
Saturday

2nd ♊

☽ v/c 6:55 am

☽ → ♋ 8:08 pm

Color of the day: Black
Incense of the day: Rue

Blessing the New Year

Call it setting a New Year's resolution. Call it forward planning. Call it setting a magical intention. Whatever you call it, it's important to call in a New Year's blessing for yourself, your community, and the planet.

Working alone or with your circle, go into your alpha state and consider what you want for the coming year. Think of yourself, but also think of your community (magical, political, civic, etc.) and the planet as a whole, including all the people and our animal and bird and other cousins who live here, too. What kind of energy do you want to draw into your life?

Now, using your forefinger as your magic wand (see January 20 if you don't know about this), draw small sunwise circles in the air in front of you. State your intention aloud, then pronounce this simple invocation:

Brand-new year—energy clear.

Good new year—energy here!

Barbara Ardinger, PhD

January 4
Sunday

2nd ♋

☽ v/c 11:53 pm

Full Moon 11:53 pm

Color of the day: Gold
Incense of the day: Juniper

Choosing Well

Sometimes all you need for better decision making is to take a moment or two to center yourself, but a little extra magical willpower doesn't hurt either. To make this willpower-promoting bracelet, you'll need about eighteen inches of 2 mm leather cording, plus either a carnelian or a turquoise bead (for courage and healthy choices) and two tiger's-eye beads (for courage and protection), all with holes big enough to fit the cording. To begin, knot one end of the cording and then make another knot about two inches farther in, then slide on a tiger's-eye bead. Follow that bead with the turquoise or carnelian bead and then the other tiger's-eye bead. Tie yet another knot after the last bead and finish with a small loop at the end. To close, simply slip the knot on the one end through the loop. As you're making your bracelet, keep your intentions firmly in mind.

Laurel Reufner

January 5
Monday

3rd ♋

Color of the day: Ivory
Incense of the day: Clary sage

Emergence Spell

With the energy of the full moon just barely behind us, this is a good time to think about the self you truly are and wish to be. Take some time to sit in meditation with a crystal suitable for programming. Into this crystal, project your ideal self, your ideal life. Allow yourself to dream big, and do not censor yourself. Next, take a skein of soft yarn and wrap the crystal round and round, round and round, until you're trancy. Then, each night until the moon is new, unwrap a portion of the thread while chanting:

My truest, most real self is emerging.

My highest, most ideal self becomes.

When the moon is new, the crystal should be fully "emerged," as should you. Keep the crystal in a pocket or medicine bag to help project the energies of your new self wherever you go.

Thuri Calafia

 January 6
Tuesday

3rd ♋

☽ → ♌ 6:03 am

Color of the day: Scarlet
Incense of the day: Basil

Refresh Your Personal Protection

It's a new year. By this time you should be over your hangover and have broken all your resolutions. You should, however, take the time to reinforce all the protection spells you have around your house, apartment, or office space.

Start with salting down your office space. Use those little salt packets you get at restaurants to sprinkle around your desk or work area. The cleaning crew will be in later to suck up all that negativity and remove it for you.

At home, put some fresh protection oil on your windows and door. Dip your finger in the oil or use chalk, and make a pentacle on all house openings. Some red brick dust will reinforce your magical protection by refusing entrance to malevolent spirits.

When refreshing your protection, don't forget to place your intent to protect your home, your loved ones, and your property into your working.

Boudica

January 7
Wednesday

3rd ♌

Color of the day: Yellow
Incense of the day: Bay laurel

The Devil Is in the Details

For this spell, assemble the following items: the Devil card from the Thoth tarot, fifteen small black candles, pure essential sandalwood oil, and semen for anointing.

In the early hours before sunrise, assemble the components and perform this tarot manifestation spell in a dark, private place. Into each of the fifteen black candles, imbue a facet of the manifestation goal at hand. Rub semen and pure essential sandalwood oil onto each candle. Place them around the Devil card. Light each candle as you speak the purpose of the spell clearly and concisely. For absolute success, try to accept the sexual act, and its fluids, as cosmic symbols of our perpetual creation. While the candles burn down, meditate on each step of your journey to manifestation. If your mind drifts, return it to your goal.

Document the process in a magical journal, and refer back to your goal-oriented magick throughout the season of gestation for results born of spring.

Estha McNevin

 # January 8
Thursday

3rd ♌

☽ v/c 12:05 pm

☽ → ♍ 5:58 pm

Color of the day: Crimson
Incense of the day: Mulberry

Releasing Through Snow and Ice

If you're lucky enough to have a little snow in your area at this time of year, it's a good idea to take advantage of the crystalline magick surrounding you. This releasing spell is particularly pertinent tonight because the winter moon has just begun waning. If snow is not at your disposal, consider doing similar magick by getting creative with ice cubes.

Take a bowl outside and collect a healthy amount of snow. Taking the bowl inside to your sacred space, make a snow sculpture to represent something you wish to release from your life. Keep the sculpture in the bowl, and place thirteen whole cloves around the sculpture. Once created, intently focus the unwanted energy into the sculpture and say:

Released in the name of the waning moon, as the Horned One rests in his wintry tomb, I hereby command this to forever flee, as I do will, so mote it be.

Raven Digitalis

January 9
Friday

3rd ♍

Color of the day: White
Incense of the day: Orchid

Magical Weather Forecasting

According to old weather lore, the weather on this day foretold the type of weather to be expected for the summer. Here's a way you can do some magical weather forecasting of your own. It's fun and can be surprising, too. You'll need your pendulum and a map. Use a professional map; a map in an atlas would be perfect. First hold your pendulum as you think of your magical intent. Then hold the pendulum over one area of the map at a time. Ask questions about the weather that can be answered with *yes* or *no*. For example, you may hold the pendulum over the East Coast as you ask: *Will there be many hurricanes this year?* Begin to move the pendulum over that area. Does the answer begin to change or stay the same? Record your observations and check back to see how accurate you were.

James Kambos

January 10
Saturday

3rd ♍

☽ v/c 10:46 am

Color of the day: Blue
Incense of the day: Ivy

Dissolution of Obstacles

Since we're ten days into the New Year and this is the time when people begin to falter in their resolutions, it's an ideal time to cast a spell for removing barriers to success. To cast this spell, write a list of specific obstacles blocking you from your chosen goal, such as "craving for chocolate," "fear of elevators," or whatever applies.

Once you have your list, light some incense composed of equal parts frankincense and myrrh in a cauldron, and light a white candle. Study your list and make sure you desire to be free of each item. Hold the list, sending your stress and worry about these obstacles into the paper. When you're ready, light the paper in the candle's flame, then drop it into the cauldron while chanting:

Banished, broken, dissolved away,

Obstacles vanish; I'm on track to stay.

Once cooled, bury the ashes and candle remains in the ground.

Michael Furie

January 11
Sunday

3rd ♍

☽ → ♎ 6:57 am

Color of the day: Yellow
Incense of the day: Almond

Channel the Comfort of Carmenta

The moon is waning, and it is quite likely that your energy may be waning from the celebrations of the past two weeks. Now is the time to increase your personal energy by giving. What we give comes back to us threefold.

Rally your family to be generous and cheerful givers to those in need. Early in the day, prepare a hearty crockpot meal. Then honour the spirit of Carmenta, a goddess of motherhood, and offer motherly comfort to others. Volunteer at a local soup kitchen. Before you leave the house, ground and center, and offer up a request for stamina.

Should actual participation not be an option for you and yours, contribute to a local food bank. Make it a group project, a scavenger hunt in the supermarket, and create several nutritious meals. This will be an educational challenge, being limited to nonperishable items. A third option is preparing several meals to be frozen and delivered to an elderly member of your community. Out of this comes an opportunity for cooking lessons. At the end of the day, your family can relax and partake of the comforting soup or stew simmering in the crockpot. Encourage all to share their favorite part of the day, or what they learned.

Emyme

NOTES:

 **January 12**
Monday

3rd ♎

Color of the day: Gray
Incense of the day: Lily

Rug Spell

Rugs decorate our homes, protect our floors, and give us a place to wipe our feet. Practical and also often pretty, rugs take a lot of abuse and absorb a lot of dirt and energy. Since the moon is waning, now is a good time for cleaning and clearing. To dispel any negative or stale energy from your living space, use this spell while you literally clean any rugs you have in your home. This spell can be used for any type of rug—large ones that you have to beat or vacuum, small ones that you can wash or shake, and even bath mats. As you wash, vacuum, beat, or shake out the rugs, visualize the cleaning as a clearing of energy. Use this chant as you clean:

Out with dirt, out with dust,

With this act, I entrust

A home that's clean, renewed, and clear—

A magic touch throughout the year.

Ember Grant

 January 13
Tuesday

3rd ♎
☽ v/c 4:46 am
4th Quarter 4:46 am
☽ → ♏ 6:44 pm

Color of the day: White
Incense of the day: Cinnamon

The Light of Lohri

Lohri is a holiday celebrated by Buddhist, Hindu, and Sikh people. Originally intended as a winter solstice celebration, the holiday has since shifted in timing and taken on additional meanings. Now it honors the end of winter, along with the harvest of rabi crops, which are sown in winter for harvest in spring. People celebrate with dancing, singing, and wearing brightly colored clothes.

Traditional foods include peanuts, sesame seeds, and butter. These represent abundance, fertility, and good health. Sweets also play a role in Lohri festivities. You may wish to look for honey-roasted peanuts or sesame candies. Clarified butter, or ghee, is marvelous for cooking because it can withstand high temperatures without burning.

Here is a blessing to say over your holiday treats before enjoying them:

Seeds of winter

Turned to spring,

Bless my magic
As I sing.

Bring abundance
To the land,
Health and honor
To my hand.

        Elizabeth Barrette

NOTES:

January 14
Wednesday

4th ♏

Color of the day: Brown
Incense of the day: Lilac

Kolam for a Cold Day

This chilly January day marks the Indian festival of Makar Sankranti, when Kolams—patterns of sacred geometry—are drawn on front stoops in colored rice powder to invoke blessings for the year ahead.

Create a Kolam in colored chalk on the sidewalk in front of your home to bring protection and abundance. Use symbols or patterns that hold meaning for you, and refer to a trusted source on color magic to decide which hues to use.

Before you draw, sweep your work space to clear it of any physical debris and cloudy energy. As you draw and color your pattern, recite an incantation of purpose to fortify your intentions. It can be as simple as:

Blessings of the sun,
come to my doorstep!

Let the wind, rain, and sun wash the drawing away and carry your request to the universe.

        Natalie Zaman

January 15
Thursday

4th ♏

☽ v/c 6:52 pm

Color of the day: Purple
Incense of the day: Balsam

Wassailing the Trees

The tradition of wassailing the apple trees goes back many centuries. Following the winter holidays, townsfolk would troop into the local apple orchards, where they would sing and drink wassail among the trees in hopes of bringing luck and fortune, frightening evil spirits from the orchard, and ensuring a bountiful crop.

To carry out your own wassailing, pour cider or ale into a tankard and head for your favorite apple trees. Once there, sing a wassailing song while circling the trees and drinking from your tankard. Pour an offering of cider or ale over the roots of each tree, repeating this traditional rhyme:

Wassaile the trees, that they may beare
you many a Plum and many a Peare;
For more or lesse fruits they will bring,
as you do give them Wassailing.

Finish your drink, circle the trees again, and depart singing or whistling.

Susan Pesznecker

January 16
Friday

4th ♏

☽ → ♐ 3:01 am

Color of the day: Coral
Incense of the day: Alder

Get Things Moving Spell

Is your spellwork taking longer than you'd like? Then let's get things moving! All you'll need is your cauldron, a rock about the size of your fist, and water.

Fill your cauldron with water, and stir three times with your hand. Next drop the rock into the cauldron—the rock represents any blockages that may be holding your spell back. Once again, stir the water as you say three times:

Things are moving,

Things are flowing.

The wait is over,

My wish is here.

Take your cauldron outside. Hold your cauldron with both hands, and swirl the water and rock around. Visualize the spell coming to fruition. End by pouring the rock and water on the ground. Walk away.

James Kambos

January 17
Saturday

4♏ ♐

☽ v/c 2:25 pm

Color of the day: Indigo
Incense of the day: Magnolia

Saint Anthony's Day Animal Blessing

Today is associated with Saint Anthony of the Desert. An often severe, volatile, and even wrathful personality, he reveals a more endearing side of his personality in his role as protector of domesticated animals. In Mexico, many church clergy encourage people to bring animals to them to be blessed. Today would be a perfect day to offer blessings upon your own animal friends. It is not necessary to bring your animals to a church to receive a blessing. Use an animal-safe holy water of your own creation, and anoint your animal with a small amount of the water while saying a blessing such as the following:

Divine blessings I do confer

To friends and family of scale, feather, fin, and fur.

Blessings to all creatures on earth near and far,

For connected through the earth we all are.

So mote it be!

Blake Octavian Blair

 # January 18
Sunday

4♏ ♐

☽ → ♑ 7:04 am

Color of the day: Orange
Incense of the day: Marigold

Reexamine Old Goals

Call on the illuminating sun and light a white candle. In a journal, brainstorm all your "I should's." Go through your mind as you would a file, looking for all the places where you tell yourself you "should," especially related to your life path. For example, you might write, "I should make more money" or "I should be more successful at _____." Then write a new list, changing every "should" to "could."

Now that you know you *could* do these things, ask yourself, "Do I really want to?" If the answer is no, gaze at the "could" statement as you tap your thymus (the sternum area between your throat and heart) lightly with your right hand as you say:

I now release this old goal
in all directions of time.

Then cross it out. If the answer is yes, note one small way you can move toward that goal within the forthcoming moon cycle, and commit to doing so.

Tess Whitehurst

January 19
Monday

4th ♑

☽ v/c 5:51 am

Color of the day: Silver
Incense of the day: Neroli

Birthday of Martin Luther King Jr. (observed)

Fasting Day for World Peace

Fasting is an act of self-discipline that inspires the body to experience a fight-or-flight hunger response. This gives us a chance to look at and then learn to control the primal aspects of our ego that we typify in esoteric culture as the shadow self. This lesser self responds only to primal sensual needs and physical gratification. To reform the chaos of reactive emotions into spiritual choice is to understand key spiritual themes of self-control. For many, celebrating civil rights and the global peace movement while fasting is one way to honor and empathize with all peoples who struggle for their own sustainable and verdant slice of global prosperity.

Beginning at sunrise, settle yourself before your home altar or shrine, and make your own prayers for peace. Express your hopes and goals for human evolution, and fast throughout the day by drinking only water and eating no food. Try to be mindful of the global consciousness and of our shared global determination to end hunger by promoting pacifism, education, and political mediation as alternatives to war. If you would like to learn more, get inspired by visiting www.thekingcenter.org, or dig deeper into the roots of Martin Luther King's inspirations by exploring the work of Mahatma Gandhi at www.gandhiinstitute.org.

Estha McNevin

Notes:

January 20
Tuesday

4th ♑

☉ → ♒ 4:43 am

☽ → ♒ 7:59 am

New Moon 8:14 am

Color of the day: Red
Incense of the day: Cedar

Pointer-Finger Magic Wand

We can carry a magic wand, but we probably don't have it at hand at all times. What we always have at hand is the oldest magic wand of all: our forefinger. The index, or pointer, finger is ruled by Jupiter. Using the index finger of your stronger hand (right if you're right-handed, left if you're left-handed), create energy by drawing little sunwise circles to create magic and draw energy toward you. To repel or unwind energy, draw little moonwise circles.

With the new moon, we usually do magical work to bring something new into our life. Consider what you want—abundance, health, creativity, etc.—and create a symbol of it. You can draw it, visualize it, or use a real physical object. With your symbol firmly in mind, begin drawing little sunwise circles with your power finger. Do this with dawn's rising energy every morning as the moon waxes.

Barbara Ardinger, PhD

 January 21
Wednesday

1st ♒

☽ v/c 8:45 pm

Color of the day: White
Incense of the day: Lavender

A Midweek Reminder from the Magician

The energies of Wednesday meld well with the tarot's major arcana card the Magician. Take an image of your favorite Magician card and place it visibly in your workspace or carry it on your person. The Magician serves as a useful midweek reminder for us that we, like the Magician, have many resources available to us at our disposal to get ourselves through the week. We simply have to remember that we have these resources and to utilize them!

At the start of your day, meditate upon the image and archetype of the Magician. Remember to call upon the energies of the Magician as needed to get you through the day and the rest of your week.

Blake Octavian Blair

January 22
Thursday

1st ♒

☽ → ♓ 7:48 am

Color of the day: Turquoise
Incense of the day: Apricot

Chasing Away Winter Blues

Winter can be the worst when it comes to health. Long, dark nights and overcast days can trigger Seasonal Affective Disorder, a depression due to the lack of sun at this time of year. It can begin as early as the fall, and drag into the winter. It is sometimes called the winter blues.

Severe depression should be treated professionally, but there are things you can do to chase those blues away. Make a connection with Helios and take full advantage of bright winter days to get outside and soak up some of those winter rays. Visit your local public greenhouse; not only will the seasonal plantings brighten up your day, but traffic to your local public garden benefits that organization.

Move your desk to a window, use bright or sheer curtains during the day to allow more sun into your home, and get out and walk in the sun.

Boudica

January 23
Friday

1st ♓

☽ v/c 6:13 am

Color of the day: Pink
Incense of the day: Cypress

Earth Elemental Spell

With Mercury in retrograde, intuition and instinct work better than words or phrases. Take a moment under this Diana's Bow moon, and meditate on the energies of earth. See mountain ridges in your mind; feel the strength and power of the earth—her body and bones, the soil and the rocks—beneath your body; smell the sacred and rich deep scents of the earth, whether clay, loam, or sand. Breathe the moist air near the snow-covered ground or rain-moistened grasses; hear the creaks and cracklings of trees and rocks as they shift and settle. Feel your own flesh and bones, and know that you are as one with the earth and all her creatures. Cast a circle in your mind and vow to honor your body today, to nurture health, and pleasure, and rest. Promise to give your body this honor from this day forward. Be blessed.

Thuri Calafia

January 24

Saturday

1st ♍ ♓

☽ → ♈ 8:31 am

Color of the day: Gray
Incense of the day: Patchouli

Renew Your Spirit Spell

It's easy to become depressed at this time of year. This spell will refresh you. First place a spice-scented candle on a table and sprinkle nutmeg around it, but don't light the candle yet. Darken the room and close the drapes. Sit in the center of the room. Breathe deeply and close your eyes. Let the darkness calm you, feel it healing you. Do this as long as you wish.

Gradually return to your everyday world. Turn on the lights, open the drapes—let the light flood the room with positive energy. Now light the candle and feel a sense of warmth and well-being return to you. You should feel a tingling sensation from your feet to your head. Sprinkle a few grains of the nutmeg over the candle's flame to release its healing properties. Burn the candle a while, then extinguish it.

James Kambos

NOTES:

January 25
Sunday

1st ♈

Color of the day: Amber
Incense of the day: Eucalyptus

Opposite Day Trait Exchange

Today is Opposite Day. This is a modern holiday, but it ties into many historical equivalents that celebrate the antics of various Trickster figures. It is customarily observed by saying the opposite of what you mean.

However, actions speak louder than words. The contrary energy of this holiday may be harnessed for changing personality traits. If you are typically hurried, try being patient. If you are often angry, act calm. If you're a pushover, be assertive for a day. Break a bad habit. See how it works for you.

Here is a charm for you to say as you begin:

Hello is goodbye, goodbye is hello.

Tell your bad habits and traits where to go.

As down becomes up, and up becomes down,

You try something new all over the town.

Now cold into hot and hot into cold,

Show what to let go and what you may hold.

Elizabeth Barrette

NOTES:

January 26

Monday

1st ♈

☽ v/c 9:23 am

☽ → ♉ 11:37 am

2nd Quarter 11:48 pm

Color of the day: Lavender
Incense of the day: Hyssop

Fire and Air Conjure Bag for Projecting Success

With the sun in Aquarius and the moon moving through Aries early in the day, this is a great time to use magic for success. A well-made conjure bag can be carried in a pocket or purse to radiate its influence while remaining inconspicuous.

A simple formula for success in your endeavors is to blend a mixture of equal parts white clover flowers and powdered ginger (you can also add an equal part cinquefoil to the mix), placing it in a yellow or orange charm bag and tying or sewing it shut. Consecrate the bag over the flame of an orange candle and in the smoke of incense composed of one part benzoin to three parts sage while saying the following to seal the spell:

Air and fire, success ignite,

Ensure good fortune, on path I am kept.

Projects and goals, inspiration takes flight,

Through this charm, I am blessed.

Carry the bag with you.

Michael Furie

NOTES:

January 27
Tuesday

2nd ♉

☽ v/c 9:18 pm

Color of the day: Black
Incense of the day: Ginger

Seven-Day Candles for Manifestation

If you've ever been to an occult shop, whether online or in person, you may have seen seven-knob candles for sale. These are especially prominent in shops catering to those who practice Vodou, Santeria, Candomble, and other religions of the African diaspora.

For our purposes, I advise either buying one of these or making your own: simply stick six needles equidistant apart along a twelve-inch taper candle. Align the color of the candle to the intention of your manifestation. Next, carve the seven symbols representing your intention onto each nub.

Perform magick by practicing visualization, meditation, spellwork, and chanting concerning the manifestation you're aiming for, while burning the uppermost nub down to the needle you inserted. Do this once a day. Use your magickal knowledge to structure solid spellwork. Continue this for seven days, and safely dispose of the wax and needles once completed.

Raven Digitalis

January 28
Wednesday

2nd ♉

☽ → ♊ 5:36 pm

Color of the day: Topaz
Incense of the day: Honeysuckle

Data Privacy Day

Currently celebrated in the United States, Canada, and more than two dozen European countries, Data Privacy Day promotes education and awareness of the importance of privacy in this ever more technological world. Originally, the focus was on teens and youth and the protection of personal information online. With the huge leap forward of social media, the focus has expanded to families, consumers, and businesses. Events this day are aimed at encouraging opportunities and dialogues among all stakeholders, large and small.

Take time today to perform a "cleansing" of personal technology. This may take the form of a simple sage smudging. You may wish to perform a complete backup of your hard drive, or perhaps delete files or data more than one or two years old. Take a look at social websites to which you belong and possibly edit your information. Light orange, yellow, and/or violet candles. Call upon Mercury as the god of communication, or whatever goddess or god you call upon for personal protection. Be sure to include a request for blessing and a thought of gratitude such as:

> Mercury, messenger of the gods, protect my thoughts and words in electronic communications.

> Help me to remain mindful of the power of the word, and not hit that "Send" button in haste or anger.

> Create barriers, allow no damaging, negative energy to enter through my computer or other devices.

> Now that it is cleansed, aid me in keeping my personal technology free of dirt, in all forms.

Emyme

NOTES:

January 29
Thursday

2nd ♊

Color of the day: White
Incense of the day: Carnation

Shoe Spell

We wear shoes every day, but how often do we take care of them, and our feet? In addition to the practical pampering—such as pedicures and massage for our feet, and waterproofing and polishing for our shoes—we can give our feet and shoes a magical boost as well. This spell can be used to break in new shoes or revitalize old ones; it's intended to be protective and rejuvenating and to bring good fortune wherever you go. Hold the shoes in your hand and visualize them cradling your feet protectively. Whatever your daily purpose—being at work, exercising, socializing, or taking an important metaphoric step in a new direction—you will be, as the saying goes, putting your best foot forward. Chant:

> Walking, running, moving on,
> Shoes empower every step.
> Feet that carry me be strong,
> In my goals I am adept.

Ember Grant

January 30
Friday

2nd ♊

☽ v/c 4:24 am

Color of the day: Purple
Incense of the day: Vanilla

Peace

Bring some peace and harmony into your life with this easy candle spell. You will need a purple candle flanked by two silver or gray ones, some blank paper, and purple ink. Ground and center, then focus your intentions on feeling peaceful and having your life more in harmony. By the light of the candles, write a list of things that you find peaceful or that promote peace within your life. Place the list under the purple candle, and allow the candle to burn down. Depending on your candleholder, some of the wax may have gotten on the paper. This should be fine. Afterward, place the list behind a mirror on the wall somewhere in your home, allowing that peace to reflect outward into your living space.

Laurel Reufner

 **January 31**
Saturday

2nd ♊

☽ → ♋ 2:09 am

Color of the day: Brown
Incense of the day: Sandalwood

Behold the Lights!

Behold the power of light, particularly in deep winter! In summer, light is brilliant and forceful, a penetrating sun-gold that lights and heats the world. But in winter, light seems to appear from the darkness and feels alive and warm, bringing subdued texture as it warms hearts and faces.

Make light an intentional part of your winter magickal workings. Candles placed in Mason jars can be safely set in windows and work perfectly as outdoor luminarias, outlining ritual space, while the same jarred candles can be carried to the ritual area, creating a moving lighted procession. A campfire or hearth fire can be used to open ritual or to toast marshmallows for cakes and ale afterward. And don't neglect strings of lights, which can be strewn indoors as well as out. Use clear lights for illumination and colored lights for specific purposes. Here's to lighting up your magicks!

Susan Pesznecker

February

February is the second and shortest month of the year. Named after the Latin word *februum*, it means "purification." This corresponds with the purification ritual of Februa on the full moon, originally the 15th in the ancient Roman calendar. Do some late-winter or early-spring cleaning. Get the whole coven involved in cleaning the covenstead.

Foreign names reveal more. In Old English, February was called Solmonath, which means "mud month," or Kale-monath, which refers to cabbage. The Slovene name Sveçan invokes Candlemas. The Finnish name Helmikuu means "month of the pearl," in which melting snow forms pearly drops of ice on the trees. In Polish this is Luty, the "month of ice," and in Czech it's Únor, when the river ice submerges. Native American names include Wolf Moon, Snow Moon, and Wind Moon.

This month is said to foreshadow the weather in the warm season. A wet February suggests a pleasant and fruitful summer. A dry, clear month hints at trouble to come. You can see echoes of this in Groundhog Day, where again foul weather predicts fair.

February honors Aradia, Brigid, and Juno Februa. It also features the Maiden Goddess and the consort God as Youth or Rogue.

Elizabeth Barrette

February 1
Sunday

2nd ♋

☽ v/c 8:37 am

Color of the day: Orange
Incense of the day: Frankincense

Shapeshifting Sketch

Today is the feast day of Saint Brigid, a goddess turned saint. She presides over many areas, including the arts, smithcraft, midwifery, and the hearth and home. She is also well known as a shapeshifter and appears in the form most appropriate for her followers.

To honor Brigid on this day, gather paper or a sketch pad, a pencil, and a candle, and proceed to your hearth or home altar. Light the candle on your altar or hearth in Brigid's honor, and invoke her in accordance with your tradition. When you feel her presence, see her in your mind's eye. Sketch how she appears to you. Don't worry about your artistic skills—what is important is your act of devotion. When finished, you can place the personalized image you created of Brigid upon your altar as both an icon and an offering. So mote it be!

Blake Octavian Blair

 # February 2
Monday

2nd ♋

☽ → ♌ 12:41 pm

Color of the day: Lavender
Incense of the day: Rosemary

Imbolc – Groundhog Day

Candlemas Cleanse

On Candlemas (the Christian holiday that coincides with Imbolc), candles were blessed in order to cleanse them and fill them with positivity. Draw upon this old tradition to clear stagnation and cleanse your spirit. Gather up any old, half-burned or forgotten candles you may have lying around. If you gather fewer than eight, obtain as many new ones as necessary to reach this number, or collect old, unwanted ones from friends. (More than eight is totally fine.) Ask the Goddess to bless each candle as you hold it in both hands and envision very bright white light filling it. Then anoint it with a tiny bit of frankincense essential oil. Arrange the candles around yourself in a circle on the ground or placed around the room. Then light them all, and sit or lie in the center as you envision all their bright positivity cleansing your body and soul.

Tess Whitehurst

February 3

Tuesday

2nd ♌

Full Moon 6:09 pm

Color of the day: Gray
Incense of the day: Geranium

Full Moon

The full moons have been given various names by different cultures, and the full moon of February includes such titles as the Quickening Moon, Storm Moon, or Ice Moon. To celebrate this event, decorate your altar with a combination of amethyst and clear quartz crystals, as well as laurel or cedar branches; burn sage or myrrh incense. Corresponding colors for this moon include shades of pale blue, lavender, and violet—and, of course, white or silver. We are on the verge of spring, so now is the time to acknowledge and prepare for the changes to come, even though they are not yet visible. Prepare your sacred space, light candles, and visualize life that is stirring in the soil, in the roots of plants, in the trunks of trees. What has been sleeping is preparing to awake. Imagine the potential you have that has perhaps gone unrecognized—tap into it. Feel the power of the Quickening Moon.

Chant:

Moonlight, stir the power within,

as the change will soon begin.

Life that courses through my veins,

Nature, too, knows growth and change.

Ember Grant

NOTES:

February 4
Wednesday

3rd ♌

☽ v/c 12:31 am

Color of the day: White
Incense of the day: Marjoram

Shamrock Power

We've just passed Imbolc, also called Brigid for the Celtic goddess (and saint) who rules poetry, fire, and smithcraft. Associated with the goddess is a humble plant called the seamróg, or shamrock. Because this plant grows almost anywhere, the learned horticultural books often call it a weed. But we know better. Consider its rhizome. It looks like an ugly, knobbly nut. It lies underground and sleeps in the darkness. And as soon as there's a hint of spring (maybe right now!), it pushes up and grows its three leaves.

Among other things, the shamrock is a symbol of abundance. Using green and gold crayons or markers, draw a large shamrock. In each leaf, list what you want or draw symbols of the abundance you want to bring into your life this spring. Keep this on your altar until mid-March, when the nurseries start selling potted shamrocks. Buy some and plant them in your garden, and watch the magic grow.

Barbara Ardinger, PhD

 February 5
Thursday

3rd ♌

☽ → ♍ 12:46 am

Color of the day: Purple
Incense of the day: Clove

Here Comes the Sun!

February, I think, is the month when the novelty of winter starts to wear thin, and it can be hard to remember that warmer days are on their way. The Sun card of the tarot is a perfect focusing tool to recharge a winter-weary soul.

Hold the Sun card in your hands and gaze at the images: the cheerful child, the golden flowers, the beaming sun. Think or speak this incantation aloud:

Every day,

Warmer,

Brighter,

Lighter.

Focus and repeat the incantation as many times as you need to hear the laughter of the child, smell the perfume of the flowers, and feel the warmth of the sun. Keep the card (or a copy of the image) in a place where you'll be able to see it. When you're feeling the winter blues, grab some sunshine and repeat the visualization as needed throughout the season.

Natalie Zaman

February 6
Friday

3rd ♏

☽ v/c 5:09 pm

Color of the day: Coral
Incense of the day: Violet

Tea Ceremony

Engage in the age-old ritual of tea. Gather some loose tea, a spoon, a tea strainer, a small teapot, a tea towel, a cup and saucer, and a treat: cheese, fruit, or the like. Set water to heat, wash your hands and face—frankincense soap works beautifully for purification—and put on clean clothes. Lay out one towel as a magickal surface, then ground, center, and lay your hands on the towel, blessing it to your purpose. Place the teapot in the north position on the cloth; tea leaves, spoon, and strainer to the south; cup and saucer east, and treat to the west. Acknowledge the four directions, making appeals as desired. Fill the teapot with hot water; spoon leaves into the strainer, place in the teapot, and steep, waiting silently. Pour the tea, murmuring a prayer of thanks and gratitude. Enjoy the tea and treat silently, pondering the blessings of the universe.

Susan Pesznecker

February 7
Saturday

3rd ♍

☽ → ♎ 1:44 pm

Color of the day: Blue
Incense of the day: Sage

Selene, Do Not Let Passion Run Away with You

As a result of different calendars and cultures, many gods and goddesses have more than one feast day attributed to them. Today is one of the days that favor Selene, who may be best known for her passion for the ever-beautiful, and ever-sleeping, Endymion. Each night she would slip down from the sky to be with him. This cautionary tale reminds us that over-the-top passion is not good under any circumstances. Passion must be tempered.

The following spell will help if you feel yourself becoming overly passionate about some object, person, or cause. Choose a candle in the color that symbolizes your obsession. If time and circumstances permit, allow the candle to burn out. If you need to extinguish it, tamp down or smother it. Say:

All things in moderation.

My passion for _____

Threatens to overtake and harm me.

As this candle burns down (is smothered),

So does passion's flame extinguish.

I am healed and whole.

Emyme

NOTES:

February 8
Sunday

3rd ♎

Color of the day: Amber
Incense of the day: Heliotrope

Quicksilver Communique

While under the influence of the adventurous and cosmic figure of the Water-Bearer (Aquarius), we have a unique opportunity to embrace our weirdest quirks as assets. This spell, inspired by the odd movements of the planet Mercury, uses our expression as a method of ensuring our own unique brand of success by giving gratitude where it is due.

Choose eight people whom you feel genuine respect for. Using a metallic silver pen on black paper, describe their influence on you and the goals or abilities that they have motivated you to pursue. Enclose each message in a silver envelope and bless it with the following invocation of Mercury, then drop the envelopes in the mail.

This passage is from Book III, Chapter 7, of *The Picatrix*, a grimoire of astrological magic that was originally written in Arabic and translated into Latin sometime around 1000 BCE. Nigel Jackson gives the following translation of an abridged excerpt:

Mercury, noble lord, you who are truthful, sensible, intelligent, you who, like the scribes, know and spread arithmetic, calculation, the science of the heavens and the earth! Hotarit in Arabian, Mercury in Latin, Haruz in Roman, Tyr in Phoenician, Meda in Indian. I conjure you in the first place, O light of truth.

Estha McNevin

Notes:

February 9

Monday

3rd ♎

☽ v/c 6:58 am

Color of the day: Silver
Incense of the day: Narcissus

Self-Loving Spell

Take a pink sheet of paper and list all the qualities you love about yourself. Then take a gray piece of paper and list all the things you don't like. When the dislike list is finished, cross off all the untruths. You know what they are—the things that someone else judged about you, or that your culture says a woman or man "should" or "shouldn't" be. Think of positive affirmations to counter all the things on the negative list as well as ways to make those positive affirmations come true. Carve a pink or pale blue candle with words and symbols of promise and love for yourself, and anoint it with rose or lavender oil mixed with a little lemon for friendship (for we are always best served by becoming our own best friends!). Just as you light the candle, say:

I am the perfect me, just as I am,
and I love myself unconditionally.
So mote it be.

Thuri Calafia

 February 10

Tuesday

3rd ♎

☽ → ♏ 2:05 am

Color of the day: Maroon
Incense of the day: Ylang-ylang

Freeze Out the Arrogance

Any of us can suffer from arrogance in one form or another. Use this super-easy spell to help you banish some of it from your life, but remember, the spell is only part of the process.

You will need one of the jacks found in the child's game, which can be found cheaply at most dollar stores. With focused intention, toss the jack into a small freezer-safe container. Fill the container with water and place in the freezer, imagining the negativity that comes with arrogance going into the container with the water. After it freezes, remove from the container and place outside somewhere away from your living space, then let the sun work its wonders. Make sure to put it somewhere safe from getting stepped on, since toy jacks aren't nice to foot bottoms. Walk away and it is done.

Laurel Reufner

February 11
Wednesday

3rd ♏

4th Quarter 10:50 pm

Color of the day: Yellow
Incense of the day: Bay laurel

Spell for Mercury Going Direct

As of today, another Mercury retrograde has come to a close. Those who follow astrology tend to believe that retrograde cycles—which are when a planet appears to be moving backward from Earth's vantage point—are times when a planet's influence tends to either turn inward or go awry.

To mark the occasion of Mercury returning to "normal," get a statue of the god Mercury (Roman), Hermes (Greek), or Thoth (Egyptian), all of whom are archetypally related. If needed, simply find a picture or painting of any of these gods and either hang it up or construct an altar.

Get a cage-free chicken egg and draw the alchemical symbol for Mercury (☿) on it with a permanent marker. Standing before the altar or image, become skyclad (nude) and allow yourself to enter a meditative state of mind. Gaze at the statue or image of the deity and repeat the following eight times:

Holy Mercury, cosmic father, I offer you this orphic egg. Please protect me and my loved ones as you exit retrograde.

Raven Digitalis

NOTES:

February 12
Thursday

4th ♏

☽ v/c 12:32 am

☽ → ♐ 11:46 am

Color of the day: White

Incense of the day: Myrhh

Freshen Your Nest Spell

Now, as birds begin to look for nesting sites, take time to freshen up your own nest with this spell. You'll need a couple of new throw pillows, a new African violet, and a new violet-colored candle. Sit on your new pillows before your altar. Light the candle and place the plant before it. Meditate on your home. Gaze at the plant and feel it releasing protection and spirituality.

Now say:

Divine Power, thank you for this place.

With this spell,

I protect my living space.

Let the candle burn down. Arrange the pillows wherever you want, and tend lovingly to your African violet. Add any other decorative accents at this time. Let your fresh new home décor remind you of this spell. Now your nest is ready for the coming season of light.

James Kambos

February 13
Friday

4th ♐

Color of the day: Rose

Incense of the day: Thyme

Baking with Unconditional Love

Today is Friday the 13th! While our mainstream culture loves to malign this date, thirteen is a powerful number with good connotations for we magickal folk.

Since this day is ruled by the planet Venus and is also the anniversary of the passing of culinary icon Julia Child in 2004, let's use today to cook up a bit of unconditional love in the kitchen. Find your favorite recipe for cinnamon sugar or lavender cookies (both herbs are associated with love) and bake up a batch of love-infused cookies. As you spoon the dough onto your cookie sheet, say an incantation aligned with your intent such as the following:

By loving hand, herb and flower,

I infuse their power

into this sweet confection

of my unconditional loving affection.

With noble intention on this 13th day,

I send perfect love to my friends and family.

Blessed be. So mote it be!

Blake Octavian Blair

February 14

Saturday

4th ♐

☽ v/c 10:15 am

☽ → ♑ 5:24 pm

Color of the day: Brown
Incense of the day: Pine

Valentine's Day

Willow Tree Love Spell

Since this day has long been associated with love and romance, the day itself now carries its own romantic aura that can be tapped into for love magic. A simple spell that you can cast is a bit of natural knot magic. Find a willow tree and lean against it while visualizing your ideal mate (not a specific person, just the type of person you desire) and asking the spirit of the tree to help bring the right person to you. When you feel ready, tie a gentle yet sturdy knot in one of the wispy, long branches, being careful not to break the branch, while saying:

Let my desire be fulfilled,

Spirit of willow, hear my plea.

Magic knot to bind my will,

Draw forth a love ideal for me.

Thank the willow tree and leave an offering of water or milk, then leave the tree without looking back.

Michael Furie

 February 15

Sunday

4th ♑

Color of the day: Gold
Incense of the day: Hyacinth

Acceptance Mudra

Mudras are yoga for your hands, tiny gestures that you can make anywhere if you need some metaphysical support. The acceptance mudra teaches how to go with the flow. It improves your connection to the universe. When you try too hard, nothing goes right. When you relax into the flow of things, they change naturally and gracefully as needed. This mudra also helps you make appropriate food choices and improves your digestion.

First, curl your index finger down against the base of itself and the thumb. Touch your thumb to the side of the pinky fingernail. Leave the other two fingers extended. The matching mantra is *Om Rum Namaha*.

Hold this position while you meditate on accepting what happens in your life. If you're doing this at home, allow ten to twenty minutes for meditation. Outside, this is an excellent mudra to hold while waiting in line at a restaurant.

Elizabeth Barrette

February 16
Monday

4th ♑
☽ v/c 3:17 pm
☽ → ♒ 7:13 pm

Color of the day: White
Incense of the day: Clary sage

Presidents' Day (observed)

Threshold Cleansing Spell

Vinegar has long been a trusted cleaning solution. It's natural and simple—an easy addition to a cleansing potion. For this spell, mix equal parts water and vinegar with a few teaspoons of lemon juice. Lemon, too, is a trusted cleaning agent and is magically associated with purification and often used for cleansing ritual tools. Allow the mixture to sit in sunlight for several hours, if possible. Use this water to clear negativity from entrances. As you sprinkle or spray it around doorways and windows, chant:

Portal, threshold, window, door—

Cleanse, refresh, clear, and restore!

Ember Grant

 # February 17
Tuesday

4th ♒

Color of the day: Black
Incense of the day: Bayberry

Mardi Gras (Fat Tuesday)

Prosperity Mulled into a Plumply Port

For this spell, assemble the following items:

- One bottle vintage port wine, rested upright at room temperature for twenty-four hours
- One hearty pinch shaved black truffle, to draw from the depths of divinity
- Eight whole cocoa beans, to fertilize eternal wealth
- One vanilla bean, sliced in quarters, to divide and multiply liquidated wealth
- One decanting bottle, to spill forth opulence into your life
- 220°F water bath

When the sun is setting, uncork and decant a bottle of vintage port slowly, yet carefully, for this spell. Heat the decanter by placing it in a pan of room-temperature water, then heat the water bath to 220°F and let rest for ten minutes. Take care that the water level of the pan matches the level of port in the decanter to keep the bottle stable in the water bath. When the port is warm, add the shaved black truffle, cocoa beans, and vanilla bean quarters. Rest the mulled port in the 220°F water bath for another ten minutes. Finally, as you serve up a warm glass of fortune to your guests this Fat Tuesday, give a hearty toast to fill the world with opulence.

Estha McNevin

NOTES:

February 18
Wednesday

4th ♒

☽ v/c 6:47 pm

New Moon 6:47 pm

☽ → ♓ 6:47 pm

☉ → ♓ 6:50 pm

Color of the day: Topaz
Incense of the day: Lavender

Ash Wednesday

Speak Well for Your Cause

As Pagans, we tend to be very open-minded about many topics. We take up the banner for our various causes and charities, and when challenged, we write and call influential people to influence their decisions to favor these causes.

We sometimes can get too unrestrained, too involved, and sometimes we cross the line—not intentionally, but because our causes are passionate topics. We sound inappropriate, which does not help our chosen cause. We get wrapped up in the emotions of the moment; we vent when we should be stating our case.

Work with Hermes, god of communication, to check your emotions and allow you to speak clearly and precisely in your quest to bring your causes to public attention. Outline your thoughts, rehearse your lines, remain calm, and speak well. Keep on topic and present yourself with dignity. You will then make the impact you desire.

Boudica

NOTES:

February 19

Thursday

1st ♓

☽ v/c 6:02 pm

Color of the day: Green
Incense of the day: Jasmine

Chinese New Year (Sheep)

Feng Shui for the Chinese New Year

One of the great gifts the Chinese have given to the world is the science of feng shui ("wind" + "water"). Magical wind + magical water = good fortune. Early spring is a good time to bring good fortune into our homes. The first thing to do is mundane housecleaning. You won't find good fortune in dirt and clutter, so tidy up.

Light red candles on your altar. (Red is feng shui's powerful, magical color.) State your intention to bring good fortune into your home. Using a red crayon or marker, make a list of eight items (8 is the power number) that mean good fortune to you, then wave your list eight times above the red candles. Keep the list and the red crayon on your altar, and hang red charms on red ribbons in all your windows. Visualize invigorating breezes and cleansing water sweeping good fortune into your home.

Barbara Ardinger, PhD

♡ **February 20**

Friday

1st ♓

☽ → ♈ 6:13 pm

Color of the day: Pink
Incense of the day: Rose

Conjure a Springtime Romance

Today, plant the seeds for a sassy springtime romance. Print out or draw tiny calendar pages for March, April, May, and June. Light a pink candle. Close your eyes and feel the feelings you'd like to feel surrounding your love life. Don't envision anyone specific—simply imagine being in the midst of the conditions you desire. Anoint the calendar pages with jasmine or rose absolute essential oil, and place them in a small glass jar with a lid. Fill the jar with organic honey as you chant:

Sweetness fills this heady time.

I call on love and lust sublime.

This springtime is the most divine.

Tightly close the lid and place on your altar. Every new and full moon, rotate it thrice in a clockwise direction. In July, release the contents in a moving body of water to keep the magic flowing in your life in the most positive of ways.

Tess Whitehurst

February 21
Saturday

1st ♈︎

☽ v/c 7:36 pm

Color of the day: Gray
Incense of the day: Rue

A Manifestation Jar

At this time of year, the sun is waxing, or increasing in strength, so it's a good time to perform manifestation spells. In my experience, the universe has a funny way of giving omens, signs, and synchronicities when they are needed most. For this manifestation jar, begin by stating your intention to the universe by communicating with your gods, guides, and guardians using the methods you are most comfortable with. Ask them to deliver significant items to you that align with the intentions you're casting.

Decorate your chosen jar with images and symbols matching your intention. Get creative and have fun; this jar is meant to be an artistic keepsake. Place pieces of paper in the jar with your wishes to the universe for things you wish to create in your life and in the lives of others. Pay careful attention to small items you may synchronistically discover in nature—even things like trinkets from shops—and add them to the jar to aid in the magick.

Raven Digitalis

 # February 22
Sunday

1st ♈︎

☽ → ♉︎ 7:28 pm

Color of the day: Yellow
Incense of the day: Eucalyptus

Last Day of the Celebration of Parentalia

Parentalia was quite a celebratory time in ancient Rome, honoring family, past and present. It lasted from February 13 to 21. The last day was called Caristia.

On this date, honor your ancestors. Create a list of those who have passed in the last few years. Find a picture of the patriarch and matriarch—the original couple or couples who gave life to your family. Start a family tree. Go back several, or many, generations. The Internet is full of websites that specialize in genealogy. Call family members in the area to help fill in any blank spots. Plan a family reunion. Perhaps make the last Sunday of every February a time for a family get-together. Burn white candles for honor. Ask attendees to bring old family photographs and a treasured family recipe. Make copies and produce photo/recipe albums for every branch. Children can fashion a family crest. Design a family blog; include the photos and download them onto flash drives.

Emyme

February 23
Monday

1st ♈ ♉

☽ v/c 9:57 pm

Color of the day: Ivory
Incense of the day: Hyssop

A Spell for Terminus

Today the ancient Romans honored Terminus, a god who presided over property lines, or the "end" of one's land. The day was frequently celebrated with neighbors. Foods served included corn, cakes, wine, honey, and meats.

Honor your own home and land with this spell. You'll need a bowl of fruit, honey, pastries, and wine and a dish of cornmeal. Begin by sprinkling a small amount of cornmeal at each corner of your property to ensure good fortune. Follow by respectfully pouring a bit of wine at each corner boundary also. Bless household spirits by placing a drop of honey at each exterior threshold. At your altar, raise the bowl of fruit as a gesture of thanks to Terminus. Then serve your family pastries of your choice. Thank your neighbors with a small gift, if you wish. A bottle of wine, sweets, or a jar of honey are good choices.

James Kambos

 # February 24
Tuesday

1st ♉

☽ → ♊ 11:54 pm

Color of the day: Scarlet
Incense of the day: Basil

Purple Hearts

Good Dragobete to you! On this Romanian holiday (akin by the barest of threads to Valentine's Day), the first herbs are gathered, as well as any snow lingering on the ground, all of which are used to make love potions. This is, after all, "the day when the birds are betrothed."

Perform a Dragobetean spell to welcome love into your life or rekindle romance in a comfortable relationship. Plant a pair of purple flowers in a pot, and name each seed for a person in the relationship. (I like to use morning glories, as they tend to twine around each other.) Chant as you plant:

Root, leaf, and vine,

Grow, twist, and twine.

Show me the love betwixt [Name] and [Name].

Nurture your flowers and watch them grow. They will reflect the relationship and where work, love, care, or coaxing needs to be done.

Natalie Zaman

February 25
Wednesday

1st ♊
2nd Quarter 12:14 pm

Color of the day: Brown
Incense of the day: Marjoram

Day of Service

It's People Power Day in the Philippines, a day associated with activism and service. Resolve on this day to step outside of your comfort zone or your usual routine to give service to those around you. Simple options might include litter removal, ivy pulling, or guerilla gardening—for instance, scattering handfuls of local (normally found in your area) wildflower seeds in vacant lots and parking strips, where they'll burst into bloom with spring's arrival.

Want to do more? Contact your local town or city government, school, or other agency, and see what needs to be done. As you work, be aware of your hands—of their strength, the work they can do, and the magick inherent in them. Imagine the collective energy and power of people working together. Embrace your place in the web.

Susan Pesznecker

February 26
Thursday

2nd ♊
☽ v/c 3:43 am

Color of the day: Crimson
Incense of the day: Mulberry

Like Minds and helpful faces

We all want to attract helpful people into our lives. There are two ways to work this bit of magic. You can leave it open to the universe to bring more folks into your life, or you can send out a call for a particular type of help. Either way, you'll need a page from a phone book or a directory—here is where you can tailor it to the type of person you're looking for—plus some small white pebbles, a planter, and a catnip plant. Bury the page in the bottom of the planter and then add the catnip on top. Make a small path of white pebbles leading from the inside edge of the planter to the plant. While doing all of this, focus on new people coming into your life. Place in a sunny location and leave for the universe to work its magic.

Laurel Reufner

February 27

Friday

2nd ♊

☽ → ♋ 7:50 am

Color of the day: Purple
Incense of the day: Mint

Loving Others Spell

Take several pieces of paper, and at the top of each one, list the name of a friend, lover, family member, or other person you hold dear. Under each person's name, write a list of all the things you value and treasure about that person. Arrange the pieces of paper in a circle on your altar. It's okay if they overlap. Then place a tealight candle on top of each of the pieces of paper and say out loud:

_____, I love you because you are_____. I wish you only love and more _____ (list the quality, so that they may be successful in becoming even more lovable).

Know that as you do so, you create a type of all-encompassing magic and that you will inherit some of these qualities too. As a great follow-up, tell these people how much you love them and why. Blessed be.

Thuri Calafia

 February 28

Saturday

2nd ♋

☽ v/c 12:53 pm

Color of the day: Black
Incense of the day: Magnolia

I Scry with My Third Eye

With a double water sign day (Sun in Pisces, Moon in Cancer) on the last day of the month, we are given an opportunity to foretell future trends or events in the coming month. A time-tested method of tapping into psychic awareness is gazing into liquid. I've spiced it up by using a psychic potion both as the gazing surface and also to drink to enhance awareness.

For the psychic potion, combine three tablespoons rose petals, two tablespoons each of thyme, yarrow, and mugwort, and three cups water in a pot, and simmer for about ten minutes. Cool for an additional ten minutes, then strain. Reserve one cup to drink (sweeten with honey if desired), and pour the remaining two cups into a black bowl or cauldron. After drinking the potion, gaze (scry) into the bowl for visions, symbols, and answers.

Michael Furie

March

March is a time of changes and a time of changelings, a time of starts and stops and renewal. This month often begins in one season and ends in another. Other months bring transitions, but March may very well bring the most radical changes. Many a blizzard has halted the commerce of a region one week of March, while sunshine and green grass and flowers overrun the week before or after.

This month being named for Mars, the god of war, means protection of self and home also figures large at this time. Ancient calendars focus on March as the start of the new year. More recently, the 15th, or the "Ides of March," brought ill fortune to Julius Caesar, and is considered by many to be unlucky. The last three days of March, long thought to be "borrowed days" of April, also call for caution. Consider doing just a little more to guard against negative energy of any sort, especially from the 10th to the 31st. A thorough house-cleaning may be in order.

In the middle of that period of caution we celebrate the vernal equinox. Ostara—the Eastern Star—is the spoke of the Wheel of the Year observed in March for earth-based believers. Paint and hide the eggs, honor the Lady with symbols of rabbits, and create your own revelry.

Emyme

March 1
Sunday

2nd ♋

☽ → ♌ 6:34 pm

Color of the day: Amber
Incense of the day: Juniper

A Thread Spell

It was once believed that on this day, pieces of wool thread left out overnight would protect the wearer from evil. The idea of these "March threads," as they were known, dates back to the Eleusinian Mysteries. This spell is based on this ancient magical belief.

For this spell, you'll need a ceremonial candle and a piece of red wool yarn about a foot long or a little shorter. Begin this spell in the early evening. Light the candle. Hold the yarn before the flame and say:

Wool thread, colored red,

Please protect me from all negativity.

Now take the yarn outside and tie it to the branch of a shrub. The next morning, wear your yarn tied around your wrist or carry it with you all day. That evening, return the yarn to the same shrub. Hopefully, the birds will use it as nest material.

James Kambos

March 2
Monday

2nd ♌

Color of the day: White
Incense of the day: Lily

Blood Binding with Crystals

To bind your deepest personal energy to a location, try gathering a number of quartz crystals. Purify the crystals by soaking them in saltwater overnight in the light of the moon. Once dried, use a sterile diabetic lancet to draw blood from the middle finger of your left hand, and place a dab of your blood on each crystal. While doing this, breathe your energy (your prana, chi, life force—call it what you will) into the stones, connecting them to your personal vibrations.

Once dried, place each crystal in a location you deem sacred. You may bury one in a special forested area, sink one in your favorite body of water, keep one on a special altar, and so on. At any point in the future, you can visualize pulling energy through the crystals from these locations, linking you to these sacred spots for as long as you intend.

Raven Digitalis

March 3

Tuesday

2nd ♌

☽ v/c 3:48 am

Color of the day: Gray
Incense of the day: Cedar

Luck Reversal

Today is Hina Matsuri, a Japanese ritual during which dolls are burned or released into moving bodies of water after absorbing the misfortune and removing the bad spirits from a household. Although modern celebrations are elaborate and specific, their origins were simpler and involved dolls made from basic materials such as straw.

Draw upon these old practices by creating a straw or paper doll to represent you and any members of your household who would like to participate. (They can make their own or you can make them, provided they give their consent.) Place the doll(s) on your altar or in a central location, and request that they symbolically absorb all negativity and ill fortune from you and your household. At the full moon (in two days), feel and sense all negativity/stagnation departing as you safely burn the dolls and then release their ashes into a moving body of water.

Tess Whitehurst

 March 4

Wednesday

2nd ♌

☽ → ♍ 6:58 am

Color of the day: Topaz
Incense of the day: Lilac

The Magick of Mail

With the advent of e-mail and text messaging, few people use "classic mail" anymore. But there is magick in letters written and sent across distance—gifts of time and energy, too.

Write a letter to a friend or loved one. Work with beautiful papers and colored inks. Write carefully, choosing your words and spilling thoughts and love onto the paper. For fun, add a pinch of glitter or confetti to the envelope before sealing it. Inscribe a protective rune on the back after sealing, and place your personal sigil (if you have one) on the front where the stamp will be placed. Adding the stamp hides the sigil and confers protection on the letter's contents. Address it and drop it into the mail, chanting:

*Not rain nor hail nor sleet nor snow
will keep this letter from where it goes.*

*Guide it through its sacred flight,
arrival in the morning light.*

Susan Pesznecker

March 5
Thursday

2nd ♍

Full Moon 1:05 pm

☽ v/c 1:36 pm

Color of the day: Crimson
Incense of the day: Apricot

Purim

Moonstone Blessing

I like to keep a blessed moonstone with my divination tools. Both Grandmother Moon herself and moonstone carry the lunar qualities of intuition and feminine power and guidance. These qualities are important to embody when performing divinations, especially for others.

Today's full moon is a perfect time to bless objects with the moon's power. Take a piece of moonstone outside and stand under the glowing moonlight—basking in her energy. Hold the stone in cupped hands, moonlight pouring over it, and say:

Grandmother Moon, please lend your blessings,

Your firm yet gentle guidance.

Let us feel your nudges through our intuition,

So that not only may we be guided,

But others may also helpfully be led.

Lend us your lunar light so that as needed it may shine day or night.

Blessed be! So mote it be!

Store the moonstone and your divination tools together so that their energy and charge may meld.

Blake Octavian Blair

NOTES:

March 6
Friday

3rd ♍

☽ → ♎ 7:52 pm

Color of the day: Pink
Incense of the day: Yarrow

Love Myself Spell

Love starts with you and spreads its magic to everything you touch. Friday is the day to work with love spells, and that love starts with you. Make a promise to yourself to start on that path to find that love. Work with Venus, who will show you how to embrace that space within you to help you love yourself. Remember, you can't love anyone else till you start loving yourself first.

Try to keep a positive spin on all that you do. Encourage yourself to be the best you can, no matter how much or how little you succeed. No matter where you are in your life, you are doing what you can with what you have, and no one can expect more than that.

Boudica

March 7
Saturday

3rd ♎

Color of the day: Blue
Incense of the day: Sandalwood

Confidence Boost

Everyone needs a little boost to their confidence every once in a while. With just a little prep work, you can trigger this spell anytime you need it with just a simple gesture—I cross my left forefinger over the middle one in a backwards finger-crossing maneuver. The visualized image you want to call upon is that of a confident you, standing straight, head up, shoulders back, with a confident, purposeful look on your face.

To program the spell, you'll want to enter into a meditative state where you create the visualization in detail and pour energy into it. Set the trigger by telling yourself that when you perform the necessary trigger, the spell will kick in with that extra energy. You'll still need to strike that confident pose on your own, but the triggering gesture should give you an extra confidence boost.

Laurel Reufner

March 8
Sunday

3rd ♎

☽ v/c 9:24 pm

Color of the day: Gold
Incense of the day: Almond

Daylight Saving Time begins at 2:00 am

Spring Forward

Daylight Saving Time reminds us to focus on the sun as it lights our lives. Turn clocks forward one hour at 2:00 am. The sun correlates to fire, the element of transformation and swift change. Spring is upon us, and change comes as fast as a fire sweeping away old dead wood.

Today is a good opportunity to make sudden, definite changes. If you want to quit something cold turkey (like switching from regular to decaffeinated coffee) or institute a new habit (like spending an hour in the gym each week), now is the time. Set clear parameters for the improvement you want to make in your life, and go for it.

Here is a charm for empowering your transformation:

Out with the old, in with the new!

Spring forward tells us what to do.

Clocks leap ahead as sun returns;

What's new springs up as the old burns.

Elizabeth Barrette

March 9
Monday

3rd ♎

☽ → ♏ 9:10 am

Color of the day: Lavender
Incense of the day: Rosemary

Melt Away Mondayness

So many folks dread Mondays—the beginning of the work week, new challenges, giving up rest. But Monday can be as positive as any other day—it just takes a change in attitude. Melt away Monday's Mondayness with this simple spell made more potent by the waning moon.

Place an ice cube in a glass. Think about what makes Monday challenging for you. Meditate on the ice cube, and put those feelings into it. Watch it melt down. Like the ice, those feelings of weariness, that Mondayness, is powerless against nature. It has no choice but to give up its form.

When the ice is completely liquefied, pour it down the drain. Or better yet, tip the water out over plants or grass so the earth can purify it further.

Repeat whenever Monday feels a bit too heavy.

Natalie Zaman

March 10
Tuesday

3rd ♏

Color of the day: White
Incense of the day: Geranium

Appeal to Father Mars for Protection

Mars was originally not a war god but an Etruscan agricultural god named Marspiter (*piter* means "father") who protected his people and his territory. Our month of March is named for him, and his sacred day is Tuesday. If you or anyone you know is in harm's way, appeal to this great, benevolent god on a Tuesday in March.

Cast your circle with red candles on your altar. State your intention to ask for protection and then call on the god:

> *Great Father Mars, I call on you for protection. [Explain in your own words what or who is threatening you.] Great Mars, as you protected your people and lands in old Rome, please come to my aid today.*

When I called on Mars for help a few years ago, he sent two legionaries that only I could see to stand on my doorstep. They took care of things quite nicely.

Barbara Ardinger, PhD

 March 11
Wednesday

3rd ♏

☽ v/c 3:46 pm
☽ → ♐ 7:30 pm

Color of the day: Brown
Incense of the day: Honeysuckle

Releasing Astral Buildup

With the Sun in Pisces and a waning Moon in Scorpio, it's an ideal day for emotional and spiritual cleansing. To begin, stand up and start a basic tree meditation, envisioning energetic roots reaching from your feet into the earth and branches reaching from your upraised arms out toward the sky.

Next, picture the moon. Envision a beam of moonlight coming down; "see" it being caught by your branches, pulling it down into you. Feel this energy cleanse you of any tension, illness, or negativity, imagining these as gray energy blobs. Visualize the moonlight gathering these blobs, then carrying them out of you and into the earth to be recycled.

Once the gray blobs are sent into the ground, pull up your roots while continuing to fill yourself with moonlight, mentally directing it to soothe and relax you. When you feel "full" of moonlight, pull in your branches, ending the meditation.

Michael Furie

March 12
Thursday

3rd ♐

Color of the day: Purple
Incense of the day: Nutmeg

Martyrdom of Hypatia, the Divine Pagan

The life of Hypatia is well documented. The dean of the Neoplatonic School of Alexandria, she was a woman of mathematics, philosophy, and astronomy. Hypatia was educated by her father, and was an important scholar and teacher in her lifetime. Her martyrdom, purportedly at the hands of a Christian mob, is quite possibly a reflection of the rise in Christianity that drove the Pagan culture underground.

Offer up blessings and gratitude today—a Pagan, humanist, and feminist holy day. Light a candle, the color of your choice, and contemplate the gifts of education and enlightenment. Send out all good thoughts and positive energy to those who reside in nations that continue to deny proper education to women. Before you retire for the night, consider the many ways Hypatia has shown herself to you during the day.

Emyme

March 13
Friday

3rd ♐
4th Quarter 1:48 pm
☽ v/c 7:11 pm

Color of the day: Coral
Incense of the day: Alder

Las Fallas Celebration Spell

In Valencia, Spain, now begins a week-long celebration, the Fallas Festival, to dispel winter and welcome the warmer season. Fireworks are often used, and there are parades, bullfights, and music. Statues called ninots are created and placed around the city. These are giant figures made of papier-mache, wood, and plaster. They are burned at the end of the week. Images include gods and goddesses, mythical creatures, fruit, and even representations of celebrities. To create your own ninot, construct a piece of art that you can destroy. This can be a drawing, poem, photo, or anything to represent change. Burn the item in a cauldron or pot on the stove. Or, if you prefer, gather some fallen leaves and burn them instead. You may chant, if you'd like:

Welcome warmer weather,

Free from winter's chill.

Changes come upon us,

Ready, come what will.

Ember Grant

March 14
Saturday

4th ♐

☽ → ♑ 2:40 am

Color of the day: Black
Incense of the day: Pine

Outpouring Spell

Take a pitcher or bowl of water out under the moon first thing this morning, as the moon will have risen in the early hours. Hold the water vessel up to the moon and the sun, allowing both the lunar and solar energies to touch and mix in the water. Say these or similar words:

Lord of the dance, guide my hands,
lay your blessing upon this water.

Lady of love, let us become, and flow
to the sound of your laughter.

While chanting, imagine a beautiful garden, your beautiful garden, thriving and bearing fruit, green and lush and healthy and strong. Pour a little of the water on the ground, in libation, then sip a little of the water yourself, in acceptance. Use the rest of it on your houseplants, plant starts, or, if in a southern climate, on your early crops.

Thuri Calafia

March 15
Sunday

4th ♑

Color of the day: Orange
Incense of the day: Marigold

Concentrating Psychic Dream Water

At 7:08 am, collect snow or water from a source near your home. Upon the vessel, draw the symbols for sun in Pisces (☉♓) and moon in Capricorn (☽♑). Place the bottle on an outdoor altar or in a sacred location, and allow it to absorb the daily emotional energy of the psychic, mystical, and dreamy sign of Pisces, as well as the evening's grounding emotional energy of driven, determined, and ambitious Capricorn.

Remove the water from its sacred location just before going to bed. Asperge all water altar tools, cups, glasses, bowls, household sinks, fish tanks, bedding, and pillows with your consecrated psychic water to inspire visions pertaining to realistic goals and true glimpses of achievable life ambitions. Be sure to use this water wisely; as you do so, it will become a vehicle for inner sight and direction. Wherever it lands, myths and dreams will be grounded into reality.

Estha McNevin

March 16
Monday

4th ♑

☽ v/c 4:02 am

☽ → ♒ 6:14 am

Color of the day: Gray

Incense of the day: Neroli

To Improve Memory

Sometimes due to stress or a hectic schedule or whatever, we have a difficult time trying to remember everything we need to do. When we find ourselves becoming increasingly forgetful, it helps to stop and take a moment to regroup and reenergize. It also helps to use a spell.

The scent of rosemary helps the memory. It is an excellent practice to cut a sprig of fresh rosemary or to brew a potion of one tablespoon dried rosemary to 1 ½ cups water, with some added lemon and honey as desired. As you either inhale the fragrance of the fresh herb or sip the brew, repeat the following:

Reason and memory; bright, clear thought,

The fog is lifted from my mind.

Renewed focus is hereby sought,

Marked improvement I now find.

Give yourself a few minutes to relax before you continue with your day.

Michael Furie

NOTES:

March 17
Tuesday

4℩ ≈

☽ v/c 2:18 pm

Color of the day: Maroon
Incense of the day: Bayberry

St. Patrick's Day

Creating Your Own Runes

For this working, pull the Hanged Man card from your tarot or oracle deck. Regardless of the deck being utilized, the Hanged Man's symbolism holds true. For many people, this card represents the Norse god Odin, or Woden, being hung upside-down on the Yggdrasil, or Nordic Tree of the Worlds, receiving the wisdom of the Runic alphabet.

Put the card on your central shrine, and ask for the god's assistance in whatever way feels most comfortable for you. Sit in silence to create your runes. Utilize a diagram of the traditional Elder Futhark to craft runes from the material of your choice. You may wish to create runic "flashcards" for study (with each rune's meaning on the back), or you may research methods of painting or even wood burning. Craft stores sell small circular pieces of wood, or you may wish to cut sections of wood from a branch. Get creative when

making this enchanted set of runes for divination and magical work.

Raven Digitalis

Notes:

March 18
Wednesday

4th ♒

☽ → ♓ 6:58 am

Color of the day: Yellow
Incense of the day: Bay laurel

Reversing Spells

To reverse a spell that you cast for yourself, you'll need a mirror and two short or small candles (you want these candles to burn down quickly into a puddle of colored wax), one red and one black. The red candle will signify the spell that was cast, and the black one will signify neutralizing the spell.

Take the mirror and spread salt on it. Light the red candle in the center of the mirror. As the red candle burns down into a puddle, contemplate reversing this spell. Focus on canceling, reversing, and neutralizing the spell. Place the black candle on top of the red wax so the black wax melts down over the red. Your intent is to smother the first spell, and the mirror with the salt reflects the magic to the black candle wax covering and neutralizing it. Once the spell is completed, take the wax and bury it.

Boudica

March 19
Thursday

4th ♓

Color of the day: Turquoise
Incense of the day: Myrrh

Saint Joseph's Day Feast

For many Sicilians, Catholics, and New Orleans residents, Saint Joseph's Day is celebrated with a feast. To express gratitude for your sustenance, to curry the favor of Saint Joseph, and to protect against poverty, bake two loaves of yeast bread containing fennel seeds, honey, and golden raisins. Create an altar to Saint Joseph near your dinner table with a red cloth and a statue or jar candle depicting his likeness. Place one loaf of bread on the altar, along with a bowl containing nineteen fava beans. Place another bowl of nineteen fava beans in the center of the dinner table. Invite your friends or family to enjoy the second loaf with a hearty, meat-free meal. Afterward, ask Saint Joseph to bless the fava bean centerpiece with the energy of abundance and luck, and then thank him heartily. The beans will then become luck-drawing charms. Bestow one upon each diner.

Tess Whitehurst

March 20
Friday

4㵮 ♓

☽ v/c 5:36 am

New Moon 5:36 am

☽ → ♈ 6:28 am

☉ → ♈ 6:45 pm

Color of the day: White
Incense of the day: Vanilla

Spring Equinox – Ostara – Solar Eclipse

New Moon, Ostara Spell

A New Moon and Ostara mean new beginnings are at hand. The possibilities of what we can do now are endless. Let this spell for Ostara inspire you to achieve all of your goals.

You'll need two hard-boiled eggs, one dyed green and one dyed yellow. The green egg represents the awakening earth, and the yellow one symbolizes the sun. You'll also need a pale green altar cloth and some fresh grass clippings.

Begin this ritual in the early morning. Instead of candles, let the morning light be your only illumination. Cover your altar with the green cloth, then sprinkle the grass over it. In the center, place the eggs. Hold the eggs as you say:

I let go of the past and all negativity.

I face the future filled with inspiration and creativity.

Later, use the eggs as an ingredient in a salad. As you eat, feel your spirit being renewed.

James Kambos

NOTES:

March 21
Saturday

1st ♈

☽ v/c 6:51 pm

Color of the day: Indigo
Incense of the day: Ivy

Naw-Rúz Reunion

Naw-Rúz is a national festival marking the Iranian New Year. This Persian tradition spans multiple religions, including Baha'i, Sufi, and Zoroastrian. Its roots are lost in history. Sources connect it with fertility, agriculture, or the defeat of a demonic army. The festival of joy and renewal lasts thirteen days.

This holiday is celebrated with gifts and feasts. Historically, debts were forgiven and prisoners freed. Now is an ideal time to make up, if there is a damaged relationship in your life. Get in touch with the person and talk it out.

For the magical part of this observation, you'll need two pieces of natural yarn such as wool. Carefully splice the ends together to make one whole piece. Then say:

What was separate is united.
What was broken is repaired.
As above, so below, so mote it be.

Carry the yarn with you when you go to make amends.

Elizabeth Barrette

March 22
Sunday

1st ♈

☽ → ♉ 6:40 am

Color of the day: Yellow
Incense of the day: Hyacinth

Briefcase Blessing

Many people carry a briefcase to and from work, but these days it's just as likely to be replaced with a laptop bag, backpack, messenger bag, or even a really big purse. Regardless of its name and shape, it holds precious items worthy of protection, and you can create a protective effect with a briefcase blessing.

Fill a small bag with protective talismans: hematite and/or obsidian, a silver dime, an acorn, a bit of cedar or juniper, a dried clove, a large pinch of salt, three small nails, and a dried chili pepper. Tie the bag closed with a square knot for safety and balance. Working at sunrise, expose and hold your case up, offering it to the rising sun and asking aloud for protective energies. Repeat with your talisman bag, then slip the talisman bag into the briefcase and allow it to remain there, exerting its protective actions.

Susan Pesznecker

March 23
Monday

1st ♉

☽ v/c 10:25 am

Color of the day: Silver
Incense of the day: Narcissus

Welcome Spring with Marzanna

In many Slavic countries, the end of winter continues to be celebrated by the drowning or burning of Marzanna, a straw effigy said to represent the goddess of death. This rite welcomes spring, brings good luck to agrarian communities, and helps ensure a good planting season and harvest. The dummy is often fashioned by young children of the town.

Use this rite to banish any bad spirits or ill will lingering about you. Gather scraps of cloth, bits of dry leaves or dead flowers from your garden, odd bits of paper, or even old newspapers or magazines. As you create the effigy (as large or small as you wish), keep your thoughts focused on ridding all that is troubling you. Infuse the dummy with these negative thoughts. When you feel the time is right, submerge your version of Marzanna in a tub of water or burn it in a fireproof container. Throw the dummy or the ashes away, outside of your home and off of your property.

Welcome spring refreshed and protected. Say:

Ill feelings and humors of winter dead,
Placed upon this poppet head.

With water or fire carried away,
Then welcome in this fine spring day.

Emyme

NOTES:

March 24
Tuesday

1st ♉

☽ → ♊ 9:23 am

Color of the day: Black
Incense of the day: Cinnamon

On Common Ground

Finding common ground on controversial or important topics can sometimes be difficult. All too often, we tend to get emotionally involved and have a hard time seeing the problem from other perspectives, or we just can't get past the differences in opinion to find the things that we do agree upon. When that happens, break out the blue, white, and brown taper candles. Tie the candles together with a piece of black ribbon, and set them on a mirror, facing upward.

Focus on having everyone involved find the common ground between them—a place from which to build. Allow the candles to burn down one inch each day until they are too short to burn further. Move the ribbon down if you need to, and be careful that it doesn't catch on fire.

Laurel Reufner

 # March 25
Wednesday

1st ♊

Color of the day: White
Incense of the day: Marjoram

Call Someone You Need to Talk to on the Magical Telephone

Wednesday is ruled by Mercury, a versatile god, one of whose jobs is communication. Is there someone with whom you really need to communicate but you think they won't "get" what you have to say? Ask Mercury to help you have a heart-to-heart talk with this person.

Cast your circle and invoke Mercury. Visualize one of those old-fashioned can-and-string toy "telephones." See the long string between the cans braided of gold, silver, and green strands and sparkling with bright yellow and blue lights. See the waves of energy traveling in both directions along the magical string.

"Ring! Ring! This is [your name]. Can we talk?" In your circle and in your imagination, use the magical telephone to talk to the person. Speak courteously and honestly. Don't call the person names or insult him or her. The next time you meet this person in "real life," follow up (politely!) on your magical telephone conversation.

Barbara Ardinger, PhD

March 26
Thursday

1st ♊

☽ v/c 8:35 am

☽ → ♋ 3:45 pm

Color of the day: Green
Incense of the day: Balsam

Chocolate Rabbit Medicine

Walk into any shop at this time of year and you're sure to find an abundance of chocolate rabbits. The rabbit is a totem that symbolizes awareness, luck, and abundance. He's a well-grounded creature connected to the earth—he's close to it, literally, and depends on it for home and protection. And chocolate… well, there's nothing that chocolate can't fix.

Purchase (or make) a warren of chocolate rabbits. Place them on your altar or in your sacred space, and bless them with this spell:

Fast feet, bright eyes,

Earthbound, earth-wise,

Quick wit, strong heart,

Rabbit, to me your gifts impart!

Store your rabbits in a cool, dry place. Take one out when you need a nip of rabbit energy. Repeat the blessing to reactivate the magic before taking it into yourself.

Natalie Zaman

March 27
Friday

1st ♋

2nd Quarter 3:43 am

Color of the day: Rose
Incense of the day: Thyme

Candle Magic

It's always worthwhile to fine-tune our candle magick, which lends itself to a myriad of magickal traditions and situations. Select a candle color and shape that match your intent. Wash your hands and meditate over your purpose, then hold the candle in your hands, allowing it to absorb your energies. If desired, carve words, runes, or sigils into the wax, then dress the candle by anointing it with essential oil. Rub oil from the top of the candle downward if working with banishings or diminishings; rub upward for manifestations and raising energy. Light the candle and intone:

Candle heat and candle smoke,

Pow'rs of magick I invoke.

Elements four and spirit bright,

Kindled in this golden light.

Enjoy your candle workings. Either allow the candle to burn itself out or snuff the flame with a snuffer. Never blow out a candle flame, as this can disrupt the energy flow.

Susan Pesznecker

March 28
Saturday

2nd ♋

☽ v/c 9:58 pm

Color of the day: Brown
Incense of the day: Patchouli

A Magickal Act of Declaration

On this day in 1986, pop musical artist Lady Gaga was born. Gaga is known for her avant-garde and eccentric public performances and her support for equality and human rights, themes touched upon in her hit song "Born This Way."

Today, wear something as an outward declaration of who you are and celebrate what makes you…you. If you are GLBT, you might wish to wear a pride bracelet or t-shirt. Similarly, perhaps you wish to wear a symbol of your faith. Do you have a cause you passionately care about and work for? Wear swag promoting the cause. Even if you cannot wear the items to work or another location out of concern for safety, job security, or other reasons, wear them under other clothing and then "let your flag fly free" in your off time in safe locations. Even a simple act of declaration is a powerful act of magick!

Blake Octavian Blair

March 29
Sunday

2nd ♋

☽ → ♌ 1:48 am

Color of the day: Gold
Incense of the day: Frankincense

Palm Sunday

Portable Circle of Protection

A regular belt can be magically charged to become an amulet of protection. It helps if the belt is already somehow attuned to protection, like having a belt buckle with a protective symbol, but this isn't mandatory. If the belt is leather, pass it through incense of frankincense and myrrh to cleanse it while thanking the animal from whence it came for its sacrifice.

When you're ready to charge the belt, light a red candle anointed with carnation oil. Have a cup of blessed saltwater ready, and light some incense of equal parts sage, basil, and bay. Hold the belt and rub a little saltwater on the buckle. Then hold the belt over the candle flame and in the incense smoke while sending white light into the belt and chanting:

Earth and water, fire and air,

The elements wrapped around me.

Every time this belt I wear,

Protected from harm, I shall be.

Michael Furie

March 30
Monday

2nd ♌

☽ v/c 9:57 am

Color of the day: White
Incense of the day: Hyssop

Crystal Sphere Meditation

This meditation can be used with any type of stone sphere—it's the shape that counts. Sit comfortably and hold the stone in your hands. Cup your hands together. Focus on the shape of the stone, the smoothness. Clear your mind and visualize the sphere as the wholeness of the world. Connect with it. As you hold it, it holds you as well. Since circles represent the connectedness of all things, imagine this sphere as a multitude of circles, symbolic of life. Breathe deeply. Do this for at least five minutes, if you can, working up to a longer duration. If chanting help you focus, repeat these words:

Circle, circle wisdom round,

Peace within the sphere abound.

Ember Grant

March 31
Tuesday

2nd ♌

☽ → ♍ 2:12 pm

Color of the day: Red
Incense of the day: Ginger

Faerie Wings Spell

Take a long walk in nature and feel the burgeoning springtime energies in your area. Open your consciousness to the awakening earth and the warm passions of all the life around you. On your way back, while still filled with the vital energies of spring, pick some flowers from your own or a willing neighbor's garden. Separate out the petals and let them dry slightly on your altar, then mix a favorite essential oil with a small amount of carrier oil (olive and almond both work well) and rub it into your hands. Fluff and mix the flower petals with your hands in order to coat them very lightly with the oil, then sprinkle them lightly with glitter if you desire. Let the petals dry completely. Use these "faery wings" in future spells whenever you need the energies of vitality and good luck. Be blessed!

Thuri Calafia

April

April is truly the deliciousness and glory of spring! In most regions, early flowers begin showing their colors as skies clear and many birds return to their homes. Humans begin spring cleanings, and everywhere, red-blooded creatures begin pairing off for the sacred dance of courtship, whether those pairings last for a lifetime or simply a few hours. This is the month of the Sacred Marriage of the Lord and the Lady, for Beltane, or May Eve, occurs at the very end of the month, on April 30th (in some traditions, it's May 1st), and Pagans everywhere begin to plan romantic and sexy activities, from private rituals involving Great Rites to large public rituals with May gads or a Maypole. Everywhere, we see couplings, new growth, fertility, and eventually, beautiful babies of all kinds.

What will you plan for your spring celebrations? Will there be May wine? It's easy to make—just throw a handful of sweet woodruff and sliced strawberries into a punch bowl with some good white wine or champagne, and let stand for the duration of your ritual. Will you plan a Maypole dance? How about a Great Rite? Whatever you choose, do it with flair and with color, and you will be honoring the glory of spring!

Thuri Calafia

April 1
Wednesday

2nd ♍

Color of the day: Yellow
Incense of the day: Honeysuckle

April Fools' Day –
All Fools' Day (Pagan)

Ugly Wednesday

Although April 1st is known universally as April Fools' Day, this year it falls on the Wednesday before Easter. In many communities this day is known as Ugly Wednesday, and begins the Easter holiday. Let us leave the fools behind and swing into action.

This spring day may be a good time to start spring cleaning. Go through your closets and cupboards to see what cleaning items you have and what you need. Discard those almost-empty containers. You will not use that last little bit, so let it go. Inspect any cleaning rags, and discard those that may be completely unredeemable and wash the rest. Create a shopping list of supplies you need to replenish. Is this the year you finally turn to a more earth-friendly line of cleaning products, or create your own? Use rags instead of paper towels?

Include larger projects not seen on your typical cleaning regimen: ceiling fans, air intake and outflow grids/grates, baseboards, corner cobwebs. Every member of the family can help. Schedule breaks and meals to keep your energy level up. Even if you can only devote an hour or two every day, by Saturday afternoon your abode should be sparkling and you may all relax for the remainder of the weekend.

Emyme

NOTES:

April 2

Thursday

2nd ♍

☽ v/c 5:01 am

Color of the day: White
Incense of the day: Carnation

Making Time Capsule Spells

Spells don't always need to be instantly woven into the universe. Some things take time. If you feel the need to create a spell, but its effects don't need to be instantaneous, you may consider creating a magickal time capsule. This is a spellcrafting addendum.

Create an original spell with materials and incantations that resonate with you. After performing your magick, wrap the contents of the spell in black cloth or tuck the piece in a dark, hidden place. When it's time to utilize its energy, return and unwrap the piece, and draw its essence into you. You may also choose to burn the spell on a fire to release its energy into reality. Another option is to sink the spell in a river when it's time for its energy to be sent into reality. Please only burn or sink spellcasting components that are natural and quickly biodegradable, as to give reverence to Mother Earth.

Raven Digitalis

 April 3

Friday

2nd ♍

☽ → ♎ 3:07 am

Color of the day: Rose
Incense of the day: Mint

Good Friday

A Lovefeast

On Good Friday, many Christian traditions focus on austerity, but the Moravians observe the day with a "lovefeast"—a traditional meal celebrating love, unity, and harmony. To hold your own love feast, play melodious music, light pink and green candles, and serve sweet pastries or buns with coffee and/or beer. You might also serve heart-opening foods such as leafy greens and sweet fruit. Invite friends and family, or keep it intimate with just your partner or household. When you sit down, declare your intention and invoke divine help by saying something like:

We call upon the Spirit of Love as we sit down to this lovefeast. Please bless our meal and our food, and may all that we think, say, and do—now and always—increase the love and harmony in the world. Thank you.

All words spoken during the meal must embody appreciation, positivity, and love.

Tess Whitehurst

April 4
Saturday

2nd ♎

🌕 Full Moon 8:06 am

☽ v/c 11:59 am

Color of the day: Brown
Incense of the day: Pine

Passover begins – Lunar Eclipse

Moon Eggs

The *Old Farmer's Almanac* calls April's full moon "Egg Moon," a nod to the promise of fertility of the spring equinox. Capture this unique and paradoxical energy—potent beginnings (the egg) and completion (full moon)—by making moon eggs. Place three eggs in a bowl of cold salt-water and take them outside. If you can, catch the reflection of the full moon in the bowl. Invoke the power of the full Egg Moon:

> Lovely Luna, full and bright,
>
> Inside gold, outside white.
>
> Reach down with your potent beams,
>
> To germinate my fondest dreams.

Eat one egg each day over the next three days. Recite the incantation and visualize the vitality embodied in the Egg Moon coming directly into you. You have the power and potential to begin any task and see it through to completion.

Natalie Zaman

April 5
Sunday

3rd ♎

☽ → ♏ 3:04 pm

Color of the day: Yellow
Incense of the day: Heliotrope

Easter

Bring Something Back to Life

According to the Gospels (Matthew 28:1–8, etc.), when Mary Magdalene went to the tomb of Jesus the teacher, she found that he was still alive. Lowercase-R "resurrection" happens all the time, especially around the spring equinox. Let's celebrate life!

Is there something in your life that seems to have died? A faded friendship? An abandoned project? Are your houseplants dying from lack of water? Go into your alpha state and see yourself standing in front of a cave whose entrance is blocked. Is it a small cave or a large one? Is it blocked by a single boulder or a landslide? Using your pointer-finger magic wand, draw moon-wise circles to unblock the cave by unwinding the blocked energy. Go inside and see what's there. Abandoned friends? A half-written book? Half-cooked dinners?

Spend as much time as you need in the cave figuring out how to resuscitate your friendships and/or projects. Bring them back to life. And water your plants.

Barbara Ardinger, PhD

NOTES:

April 6
Monday

3rd ♏

Color of the day: Gray
Incense of the day: Clary sage

A Soil Spell

This spell is a blessing for garden soil and all the plants you grow. The items you'll need are two candles (one brown and one green), the Empress card from the tarot, some dried basil, and a dish of soil from your garden.

On your altar, place the candles, and between them lay the Empress card. In front of the card, set the dish of garden soil, sprinkled with a small amount of dried basil. Light the candles and look intently at the Empress card. She is the Earth Mother and holds the power of creation, fertility, and bounty. Now stir the basil and soil together with your hand. Basil is a superb protective herb. Hold the dish of soil and say:

Earth Mother, life giver and protector of seeds,

Bless my garden's soil,

And give me all that I need.

End by sprinkling the soil over the garden.

James Kambos

April 7
Tuesday

3rd ♏

☽ v/c 4:42 pm

Color of the day: White
Incense of the day: Ylang-ylang

Bridget's Bedded Bulbs

The early spring is a time viewed as exceptionally sacred to the Highland peoples of our planet. Our endurance of the long, dark days of winter is rewarded with the rebirth and renewal of life. For many Celtic cultures, this was a time especially sacred to the goddess Bridget, ruler of medicine, mead, and mortality. This spell draws on the Spring Goddess in all her fertile glory as she is cosmologically regenerated in the rapture of the season.

Assemble these items:

• One bottle honey mead

• Four used tea bags

• One tablespoon molasses

• Three cups warm water

Combine all of the ingredients into a one-gallon jug. Shake the jug throughout your home and garden as you chant:

Trinity ever be, the renewal of fertility.
O vivacious Bridget, by this willing
poetry, does my own strength undulate
in time with thee.

When the mixture is fully foamy, use it as plant and garden fertilizer. Pour a tablespoon at a time into watering containers, and water over the bulbs in your garden or ones that you may have potted in the house for the spring season. Each time you water, remember Bridget, our Lady of Spring, and her trinity of fertility.

Estha McNevin

NOTES:

April 8
Wednesday

3rd ♏

☽ → ♐ 1:08 am

Color of the day: Brown
Incense of the day: Lavender

Charm for Safety During Travel

Before embarking on a journey, it is a good idea to recite a verbal charm in order to give everything clear purpose and keep the energy aligned with safety and success. Before you set out on your trip, visualize your destination and see yourself in that place. Infuse into your visualization the relaxed feeling that you arrived there without any problem. When you feel ready, say this chant to seal the spell:

My journey on the path is clear,

Assured of safety and success.

I tread my road without great fear,

My trip is smooth and free of stress.

Michael Furie

April 9
Thursday

3rd ♐

☽ v/c 1:42 pm

Color of the day: Purple
Incense of the day: Clove

Magical Manicure

Help increase your bottom line with this fun little beauty spell. You will need a bottle of green nail polish in a shade you like, as well as a bottle of base coat. To give the spell even greater oomph, you will also need three pebbles small enough to fit in the opening of the nail polish bottle, plus a bottle of gold polish. Paint the pebbles with the gold polish, creating little golden nuggets. Drop the dried pebbles into the bottle while envisioning their golden color drawing more prosperity in your direction. As the final step, you will need to paint your fingernails. Start with the base coat to keep from accidentally staining your nails green. I like to use three coats of color, imagining an invisible dollar sign with each swipe of the brush.

Laurel Reufner

April 10

Friday

3rd ♐

☽ → ♑ 8:47 am

Color of the day: Pink
Incense of the day: Orchid

Revealing Your Sexy Self Spell

For this spell, you'll need seven pieces of soft thin cloth, such as silk, as well as a poppet. For the poppet, just cut out two matching gingerbread shapes from white cotton, and decorate one of them to look like yourself at your best. Sew the two pieces right sides together, then turn right-side out. Leave a gap for stuffing with herbs of love and lust, such as rose petals, damiana, and patchouli (look this one up!), as well as herbs of wisdom, such as sage and sunflower, adding angelica, if desired, for psychic visions. Sew the opening shut.

When the poppet is all finished, wrap it with the seven cloths while pondering the many ways you have been kept from being your truest sexual self. Then every night leading up to the new moon, pull one layer of cloth off of the poppet, saying:

*As I pull away this layer of [cloth],
so I open myself to the truth of who
I am, with acceptance and love.*

On the last night before the new moon, pick up the poppet and hold it close, telling yourself that you love and approve of yourself in ALL your many facets. Place the poppet on your altar, and leave it there through Beltane, to be honored and celebrated with respect and joy. Blessed be.

Thuri Calafia

NOTES:

April 11
Saturday

3rd ♑
4th Quarter 11:44 pm

Color of the day: Black
Incense of the day: Sage

Passover ends

Oracle Spell

On this day, people once traveled to seek the wisdom of the Roman goddess Fortuna, ruler of destiny and good fortune. Her temple at Praeneste was one of the largest in Italy. The modern city of Palestrina resides in that area now. Fortuna was reputed to be a powerful oracle. Visitors would draw random pieces of oakwood from a jar. Each contained a message printed upon it. The message would offer advice or a prediction, sort of like our modern fortune cookie. In honor of this day, here's a divination spell.

Draw a card at random from your favorite tarot deck. The image on the card is your oracle for the day. Watch for signs throughout the day that reveal a connection to the message that card contains. Place it under your pillow or mattress tonight, and see if you receive insight through your dreams.

Ember Grant

April 12
Sunday

4th ♑
☽ v/c 4:15 am
☽ → ♒ 1:44 pm

Color of the day: Amber
Incense of the day: Eucalyptus

Anise for Awareness

Anise is an herb of the air element, ruled by Jupiter. This masculine plant has a sharp, spicy aroma. It aids awareness, psychic power, and concentration. The element of air is connected to matters of creativity and inspiration.

Use this spell if you need new ideas for any craft. Ideally, cast the spell at night under Jupiter. You will need anise oil and an object representing your craft. Anoint the craft item with the oil, saying:

I bless my work with the power of air.

Dab oil on your wrists, saying:

I bless my hands with precision.

Anoint your forehead, saying:

I bless my mind with inspiration.

Concentrate on what you wish to receive from the element of air.

After casting this spell, keep the anointed object in your workplace. When you want a boost of inspiration, put some anise oil on your wrist where you can sniff it as needed.

Elizabeth Barrette

April 13
Monday

4th ≈

Color of the day: Silver
Incense of the day: Lily

A Magickal Act of Creation

On this date in 1870, the New York Metropolitan Museum of Art was founded. Today, in honor of this world-renowned institution and the prized works within it, engage in a magickal act of creation and exercise your artistic powers. Think of a goal you would like to work toward achieving and symbols that represent that goal. Gather simple art supplies you already have around the house, such as glue, scissors, colored pencils, paints, etc., then situate yourself in a place where you feel energetically comfortable to create. Envision the end result of your goal, as if you have already achieved it. While holding this intentional vision, make a collage, drawing, painting, or other work of art containing images and symbols relating to this goal. When you are finished, you can hang your creation where you will see it regularly to remind you of your intentions and goals in progress.

Blake Octavian Blair

April 14
Tuesday

4th ≈

☽ v/c 3:45 pm

☽ → ♓ 4:12 pm

Color of the day: Maroon
Incense of the day: Basil

Happy New Year, Eastern Style

April 14th marks the arrival of New Year festivals in many of the Southeast Asian cultures and in Japan, and what better time to mark a fresh start than in spring, the time of new beginnings!

Drape your altar with soft, silken clothes in springy pastel colors. Set out photographs or tokens to represent your ancestors, for all of your new beginnings spring from their loins. On a small piece of paper—use birch bark if you have it available—write your hopes and dreams for the new year; tie with a gold thread, and set upon the altar. Light a golden candle and meditate upon your plans. Offer thanks, wish yourself a happy New Year, and feast on rice and a bit of fish.

Allow the scroll to remain on your altar throughout the year. Open it one year later, and see how your plans have reached fruition.

Susan Pesznecker

April 15
Wednesday

4th ♓

☽ v/c 5:37 pm

Color of the day: Topaz
Incense of the day: Lilac

Sharing Is a Good Idea

O dreaded day! Did you pay your income tax on time? Here's something to consider: when we're fortunate enough to earn enough to pay taxes, we should remember what tax revenues bring us—food inspection, infrastructure repair, environmental protections, and more. When we earn enough to pay taxes, we're also fortunate enough to be able to share with less fortunate people.

Go into your alpha state and meet Dame Fortuna, she who holds the wheel of fortune and the rudder of our life. Ask her to show you where you're standing on her wheel and to help you understand where you're headed. Ask her to show you charities and organizations to which you can make donations.

Because the Great Goddess is the grandmother of the gods, we are all kin. Vow to share your good fortune. Vow to write a check to a nonprofit organization on the first of every month.

Barbara Ardinger, PhD

NOTES:

April 16
Thursday

4th ♓

☽ → ♈ 5:00 pm

Color of the day: White
Incense of the day: Jasmine

Spirit Seed Spiral

Sometimes we forget how valuable and irreplaceable we are. To ease periods of self-doubt, plant a spiral mandala of lavender. The purple flowers represent the crown chakra. Sown in a helix, they will help reinforce your connection to the Divine, and thus your belief in yourself.

Fill a round pot with soil. Take a fingerfull of seeds and, starting from the center, drop them in a loose outward spiral to the pot's edge. Then retrace the spiral, moving inward with these words:

Me to crown,

Crown to me,

Together, unsevered,

So mote it be!

Cover the seeds with earth. Repeat the invocation as you tend your flowers. Watch them—and your confidence—grow. (If your plants don't thrive, don't worry. They have absorbed your troubles. Scatter the earth and begin again.) Make small bundles of the lavender to tuck in your pocket or purse to remind you of the connection.

Natalie Zaman

NOTES:

April 17
Friday

4th ♈

Color of the day: Coral
Incense of the day: Cypress

Cultivating Friendship

Friendship knows no limits or boundaries. True friends will be there beside you no matter what happens to them or to you. Finding a friend will be a tough task, as many people will present themselves as friends. But the test of time will eliminate fair-weather friends, and only good friends will remain.

The best way to keep a good friend is to be one. Times are tough for all of us, and weathering these hard times will give us opportunities to prove our friendship. This could be an opportunity for you to show how much you care for your friends. A kind word, a helping hand, and time given without the concern of any return are the best ways to show each other that your relationship as friends is a serious commitment. Make a friend, be a friend, and share with your friends.

Boudica

April 18
Saturday

4th ♈

☽ v/c 2:57 pm
New Moon 2:57 pm
☽ → ♉ 5:31 pm

Color of the day: Blue
Incense of the day: Sandalwood

The Bowl of Reception

The new moon marks a time of beginnings and receptivity. Honor the Maiden Goddess, whose color is white and whose season is spring. View the future with optimism and faith.

For this spell, you will need an empty white bowl, a piece of paper, and a pen. Begin by clearing and consecrating space as you usually do. Write down three things that you want to bring into your life—one personal, one practical, and one mystical—such as hope, a new job, and psychic awareness. Put the paper in the bowl. Hold the bowl in your hands, and pray or meditate on the nature of receptivity.

During the next lunar month, whenever you experience something from your receptivity list, add a symbol of it to the bowl. At the end of the month, look over all the things in the bowl and give thanks for what you have received.

Elizabeth Barrette

April 19
Sunday

1st ♉

☽ v/c 7:07 pm

Color of the day: Orange
Incense of the day: Frankincense

Dressed for Success

Today is the birthday of now-deceased celebrity hairdresser Kenneth Battelle. He was noted for being the hairdresser of such famous and confident figures as Marilyn Monroe and Jacqueline Kennedy. It is also no secret that looking good in our own eyes is its own kind of magick and instills and boosts our self-confidence.

Today, dress and groom yourself in a way that is pleasing to you and that you feel expresses your own personal beauty (remembering that we all possess beauty!). As part of your process, empower a favorite piece of magickal jewelry with the goal of feeling beautiful and self-confident. Take stock of how you feel as you conduct your day, acknowledging how you may be presenting yourself differently in the world around you—with beauty and confidence (remember, operating with confidence is different from operating with ego). Self-confidence also boosts our own magickal power and ability to focus energy.

Blake Octavian Blair

April 20
Monday

1st ♉

☉ → ♉ 5:42 am

☽ → ♊ 7:28 pm

Color of the day: Ivory
Incense of the day: Neroli

Frighten Away Evil

In honor of the annual Japanese Drum Festival, make some noise today. If you own a drum, play it. If not, make your own "music" another way. Ring bells, bang on pots and pans, or even sing and shout. Use the sound to clear the air of negativity. Visualize the sounds chasing away any unwanted energy. This spell can also be used to cleanse a new living space or automobile. Simply fill the area with sounds.

Chant:

Ring the bell and beat the drum,

Singing, chanting, whistle, hum.

Banish back to where you're from,

Unwanted energy, succumb!

Ember Grant

April 21
Tuesday

1st ♊

Color of the day: Gray
Incense of the day: Ginger

Kartini Day

Today, Indonesia celebrates the too-brief yet poignant and culture-changing life of Princess Raden Ajeng Kartini. Born on this day in 1879, she opened a school and began educating girls, something that was unheard of at the time. In fact, Indonesian girls were forbidden to leave their homes before marriage.

Honor Princess Kartini today, further her ongoing legacy of feminism and human rights, and bring her activist spirit into your heart and life by lighting a white candle in her honor. Relax, breathe, close your eyes, and envision the bright white light of peace, kindness, and liberation emanating from your heart and expanding until it surrounds the planet. When this feels complete, take a concrete action in the physical world, such as signing an online petition or donating a small amount of money (even one dollar) to a charity that supports women and girls—especially one related to education.

Tess Whitehurst

April 22
Wednesday

1st ♊
☽ v/c 1:38 am

Color of the day: Yellow
Incense of the day: Bay laurel

Earth Day

Blessing the Earth Spell

This Earth Day, give back something of yourself for all Mother Earth has given you. Take a notepad and a large water container, and go out to a favorite place in nature. Sit comfortably with your back against a tree, and meditate deeply on the energies of the earth. Ground deeply and well, giving of your self, your heart, and your spirit to this wondrous organism who sustains us. Ask her what she needs in order to best grow and heal. Open yourself to whatever messages she reveals to you, and be sure not to make any promises you can't or won't keep. After your meditation, write down the relevant pieces of your conversation. Give an offering of water to the plants in the area before you leave, and then make a plan to do whatever you agreed to help her with, open-heartedly and with love.

Thuri Calafia

April 23
Thursday

1st ♊

☽ → ♋ 12:25 am

Color of the day: Crimson
Incense of the day: Apricot

Change Your Appearance Spell

The weather is getting warmer and summer will be here soon. Is there something about your appearance you wish to change? If you're concerned about how you'll look in your summer clothes or swimwear, this spell will help you.

Firmly pack garden soil into a flowerpot saucer. In the soil trace an outline of what it is you'd like to change about yourself. Next, fill a watering can with water. Pour the water onto the image you've traced. Watch as it fades. Keep watering until the soil turns to mud. Pour the mud onto the ground and rinse the saucer until it's clean. See your current appearance draining away harmlessly into the earth. Then announce in a clear voice:

The image in my mind

Is the image I shall find!

Now take the steps to change your appearance. Remember seeing the old you dissolving before your eyes.

James Kambos

April 24
Friday

1st ♋

☽ v/c 1:04 pm

Color of the day: White
Incense of the day: Violet

A Gift for the Gnomes

I am a Witch who uses stones and crystals, but there are those who do not. In fact, some Witches feel so strongly about the mining methods used to gather stones that they'd prefer we all stop buying them (because of the damage to the earth). I feel that as long as I show proper respect, there is nothing wrong with using a limited number of crystals in my personal practice.

A good way to give something back is to charge a quartz crystal with healing energy and bury it in the ground as an offering to the earth, the gnomes, and all of the spirits of the land. You can also pour an offering of cream or milk onto the ground where you bury the crystal. If done with a pure heart, this will keep you on good terms with the earth faeries.

Michael Furie

April 25

Saturday

1st ♋

☽ → ♌ 9:13 am

2nd Quarter 7:55 pm

Color of the day: Indigo
Incense of the day: Ivy

Clay-Carving Your Wishes

As the springtime sun increases in strength, we have the opportunity to weave our manifestations into reality with much greater ease.

Purchase some all-natural clay from an art supply shop. Surround yourself with eight orange or white candles to represent Mercury, the planet of communication, mysticism, and travel between the worlds. Take a small amount of clay and flatten it into a tablet of any size, with a thickness of approximately half an inch. Taking a carving instrument, draw the alchemical symbol for Mercury (☿) on each corner of the tablet and ask him to bless your endeavor. Carve symbols, pictures, and words on the tablet that are aligned with your manifestation.

Visualize your intentions becoming real while you anoint the tablet with pure olive oil. Perform any additional spellwork at this time, and allow the tablet to dry for one lunar cycle. When finished, bury the tablet on your property to seal the energy into your environment.

Raven Digitalis

NOTES:

April 26
Sunday

2nd ♌

Color of the day: Amber
Incense of the day: Marigold

Birth Date of John James Audubon

"The nature of the place—whether high or low, moist or dry, whether sloping north or south, or bearing tall trees or low shrubs—generally gives hint as to its inhabitants."
—John James Audubon

Earth-based belief systems are by definition in tune with nature. Birds hold a special symbolic place for many. Several years ago during a family reunion, I was intrigued by a relative who could recognize birds from their calls alone. This inspired me to obtain bird identification books for my specific state and area. I began recording the birds visiting my backyard. This in turn has led to many relaxing hours observing the birdfeeders and their guests from my patio.

Today, the celebration of the birth of Audubon, consider starting a bird watching, or birding, practice. You may wish to seek out local birding clubs in your community, or simply identify the birds in your own backyard. House and feeder systems range from minimal and inexpensive to complicated and luxurious. There is something in every price range;

likewise with books and binoculars. A warning, though: it can become addictive!

Emyme

NOTES:

April 27
Monday

2nd ♌

☽ v/c 10:12 am

☽ → ♍ 9:07 pm

Color of the day: Lavender

Incense of the day: Hyssop

Snapdragon and Toadflax Buried Treasure

Procure snapdragon and toadflax plants from a garden supply center. Pick a place in your garden that is special to you. In a small wooden box, stash a fresh $100 bill, your favorite pieces of jewelry, and any small trinkets that are valuable treasures to you. Bury these in the same hole you dig for the snapdragons, and just a few inches away, bury the toadflax to keep your dragons company. Both will flower into long shoots of colorful heads. They will guard your wealth and treasure while blessing it for the season.

In autumn, your investment and patience will ensure a prosperous harvest when you dig up your treasure as you clear the garden. If you have children, consider involving them in your magick by drawing a map and asking them to locate the treasure or burying special harvest treasures just for them.

Estha McNevin

April 28
Tuesday

2nd ♍

Color of the day: Red

Incense of the day: Bayberry

Elemental Garden Blessings

Today starts the Floralia (held in honor of the Sabine fertility goddess Flora), making it a great time to do some garden magic. You will need five stones to represent earth, air, fire, water, and spirit. You are going to bury each stone at the appropriate compass point after charging it with that element's life-supporting properties. Start in the north with earth, and continue clockwise with air, fire, and water. Finish in the middle with the stone you chose for spirit. It is done.

The nice thing about this ritual is the adaptability. If you have small herbs and veggies tucked in all over the place, then consider the garden area all of your yard and bury the spirit stone as close as you can get to the center. If you have to garden inside, use potted plants to hold the stones.

Laurel Reufner

April 29
Wednesday

2nd ♍

Color of the day: White
Incense of the day: Honeysuckle

Stimulating Creativity

We all have the ability to be creative. With some of us, it is obvious. But we all have a little something within us that is just waiting for us to crack open our abilities and let it out.

Each of us has something we can do better than anything else we do. It may not be much, but it is the most creative thing we can do, and each time we do it, it releases a little joy and some pride in what we have accomplished.

All we need is a little spark to push us to do the best we can. And all that is needed to make it blossom is a little attention to that spark. Find out what you are good at, and take it to the next level. All it has to do to be successful is make you feel like you accomplished something.

Boudica

April 30
Thursday

2nd ♍

☽ v/c 8:23 am

☽ → ♎ 10:03 am

Color of the day: Turquoise
Incense of the day: Nutmeg

Living Water

Our blood, our tears, and our bodies' very tissues are all made from water. The water element is the life-giver, essential to our health and to our very existence. The Elder Pliny described it as the "cause of all things that grow on Earth." The water element is cleansing, healing, and inspiring, and gifts us with psychic tools and divination skills.

Spend a day (or longer) focusing deeply on your connection to the water element. Dress in beach clothes or robes in blues and greens—and don't forget the flip-flops! Carry agate, coral, lapis, or pearls, and surround yourselves with shells, sea glass, and a bowl of sand to work with your fingers. Spend a day beside moving water, such as a local stream, river, lake, or sea. Create small "boats" from leaves or bits of wood; write your wishes on them and cast them into the current. Bon voyage!

Susan Pesznecker

Anciently, in Western Europe, the year was divided in two: the dark half of the year, which begins at Samhain (October 31) and lasts until May Eve, and the light half, which begins at Beltane (May 1). The light half of the year is the more active time, when the energy of life is strong and waxing and we can look forward to the promise of summer. Since May begins one of the halves of the year, it is an initiator; similar to a cardinal zodiac sign, it shifts power to the new dynamic. The dynamic of May is one of fertility in plants and animals (including humans), birth, growth, and abundance. Of course, in the Southern Hemisphere, the opposite is true: May is the month that ushers in the dark half of the year, the time of rest, reflection, and renewal. Either way, the month of May is an important door-way into the second half of the year and a major energy shift. It is the polar opposite of its November counterpart in a beautiful dance similar to the concept of Yin and Yang, which is a wonderful focus for meditation.

Michael Furie

May 1
Friday

2nd ♎

Color of the day: Coral
Incense of the day: Rose

Beltane

Beltane Fire Celebration

Fires are a Beltane tradition so make some sparks tonight! Take advantage of a fire pit if you have one, or make a small fire in a cauldron or candle holder and burn some small twigs or bits of paper. Honor the element of fire and its power to transform and change. The nature of the fire element is purifying, cleansing, energetic, and forceful, but it can also be destructive, so we must always treat it with respect. This time of year, the focus is on the fertile earth and the awakening of the land. Chant over your flames and celebrate the season:

Beltane fire, burning bright,

Bringing magic to the night.

Honored be the sacred flames,

Power still when ash remains.

Save some of the cooled ash from your fire and sprinkle it around the outside of your home for protection.

Ember Grant

May 2
Saturday

2nd ♎

☽ v/c 10:03 am

☽ → ♏ 9:47 pm

Color of the day: Indigo
Incense of the day: Rue

Happy Bird Day – A Gratitude Spell

It's easier to manifest things you want when you are happy with what you have. The positive energy you put out with the following spell will spread and return to you with a little help from the birds.

Collect any ribbon, yarn, and thread you have on hand, and cut them into pieces that are three to five inches long. Pick up each individual strand and run it through your fingers. As you do, speak aloud:

I am so grateful for [Name one thing you are thankful for, small or large!].

When you've embedded gratitude into each string, collect them into a basket and put them outside (or you can put the basket in a bird or animal feeder). The birds will come and take pieces of string to build their nests—spreading your gratitude and positive attitude. Get ready for good things to happen!

Natalie Zaman

May 3
Sunday

2nd ♏

Full Moon 11:42 pm

Color of the day: Gold
Incense of the day: Juniper

Spring Fever Mojo

The full Scorpio moon is uniquely suited to spring fever, or experiencing the reawakening of one's body along with the reawakening of the earth. And this comes with added benefits, such as charm, magnetism, and general enjoyment of life ("mojo"). For this purpose, create a sensual mood after the sun goes down. Turn down the lights, diffuse a sensual fragrance (such as jasmine), and have a tasty treat on hand (such as chocolate). Wear something sexy and play some sensual tunes. Then slowly begin to let your body begin to move. Dissolve into all five senses and swirl them all together: Run your hands over your skin, or the floor, or the wall. Inhale the scent in the air. Surrender to the sound of the music. Let your eyes feast on your beautiful image in the mirror. Periodically let the chocolate (or other treat) melt luxuriously in your mouth.

Tess Whitehurst

May 4
Monday

3rd ♏

☽ v/c 9:49 pm

Color of the day: Ivory
Incense of the day: Rosemary

Blessing or Protection

Select a figure of the goddess or god you want to invoke. Pick up five stones. These can be river pebbles, semi-precious gems in colors corresponding to the elements/directions, or pretty rocks you've found. Cast your circle with your altar in the center and state your intention, which can be anything from blessing the altar itself to starting some work in your community.

Now "draw" a pentacle of stones. Starting at the top of the pentacle (behind your god/dess), invoke spirit to your altar and lay the first stone down. Going from top to lower left and on around, continue drawing the pentacle with stones, invoking the elemental powers of the directions. When the pentacle is closed (use your pointer-finger magic wand to draw the lines), address the god/dess and repeat your intention. Open your circle and know that the god/dess in the stone pentacle will respond to your request.

Barbara Ardinger, PhD

May 5
Tuesday

3rd ♏

☽ → ♐ 7:13 am

Color of the day: Black
Incense of the day: Cedar

Cinco de Mayo

American Continental heritage Magic

A heritage or ancestral bowl is a Native Pueblo symbol of family, tribe, community, and humanity all contained within the vessel of Mother Earth. Honor this cultural heritage of diversity today by creating your own heritage magic. In a small wooden, silver, or copper bowl, place dried wild rice to represent the ancient peoples of our continent, beans and oats to represent our colonial ancestors, and dried nuts, peppers, and fruits to represent our own generation and time. This heritage bowl is evocative of the wealth and bounty we evoke when all of our family, tribal, and community members feel that diverse opinions and cultures are celebrated with honor and curiosity.

Display this bowl on your family mantel or ancestor altar, in honor of the courage and optimism inspired by Central American culture throughout our modern history. Mexican mariachi music, dancing, feasting, parties, and parades are the exciting ways we honor this heritage of diversity today. Commemorate this path to peace as you assemble your own heritage bowl.

Estha McNevin

NOTES:

May 6
Wednesday

3rd ♐

Color of the day: Brown
Incense of the day: Lilac

Spell to Ease Pain

Most pain is due to some form of inflammation. To help reduce this inflammation, it is useful to work with energy and color. Close your eyes and visualize red-orange light coming down into you and traveling to the site of the pain to heal the area. After a few minutes of this, shift to ice-blue light, and send it to the site of the pain to offer cool healing to ease the inflammation.

After you have finished sending the energy, sit for a time in quiet meditation and make sure all your muscles are relaxed. The more relaxed you are, the better. This exercise should be repeated often until the pain is gone.

Michael Furie

May 7
Thursday

3rd ♐

☽ v/c 1:51 pm

☽ → ♑ 2:16 pm

Color of the day: Crimson
Incense of the day: Myrhh

Goddesses of Wealth and Prosperity

Most of us could use a little help with our finances. There are many gods and goddesses associated with money, and sometimes working with them may help stretch your available funds just a little further.

The Romans had several, but the best known were Abundantia, goddess of abundance, and Moneta, goddess of wealth and prosperity. You can find their likenesses on Roman coinage. Abundantia was so popular that she actually made it into Christian sainthood. She became the Saint of Wealth and Good Fortune. Moneta started out as the Greek goddess of memory and mother of the Muses and became Juno Moneta, protectress of money under the Romans. Our own modern word *money* comes from this root word.

Remembering these goddesses in times of financial need can only help. Place a coin on your altar in their memory to ask for their help.

Boudica

May 8
Friday

3rd ♑

Color of the day: White
Incense of the day: Alder

White Lotus Day

It's White Lotus Day, a day celebrated worldwide by theosophists in commemoration of the death of noted theosophist Helena Petrovna Blavatsky in 1891. Theosophy is a philosophical system that finds links between nature, divinity, and enlightenment. On May 8th, theosophists meditate on the metaphor of the lotus, a flower that emerges from mud, grows through water, and emerges into the glory of air and sun, symbolizing spiritual accomplishment. The lotus is believed to represent the four elements in pure form, and it is a thing of perfect beauty besides.

Find a simple image of a lotus in a book or on the Web. With paper and pencil, draw the lotus's shape and then reflect, tracing the lines repeatedly as you consider how the lotus applies to you. What "mud" must you find your way through in order to emerge into the light of day? Contemplate the lotus and gather strength.

Susan Pesznecker

 ## May 9
Saturday

3rd ♑

☽ v/c 4:35 pm

☽ → ♒ 7:22 pm

Color of the day: Gray
Incense of the day: Patchouli

Practical Glamoury for Confidence

Positive affirmations can go a long way when we are feeling insecure or unconfident. Sometimes our jobs or social obligations force us to enter the public sphere even when we don't feel like engaging.

To help boost your confidence, situate yourself in front of your bathroom mirror. Looking deeply into your own eyes, repeat the following out loud many times, and then silently in your mind afterward:

I am formed in perfect beauty. I embody health through body and mind. I am at peace. I am at ease. I embody strength.

If you wear makeup or lotion, take a few moments to envision the product surrounded by a radiant glow, like little stars or suns. When you apply the product, see your body as the canvas and the product as a type of celestial paint, lending you limitless strength and courage. You may also choose to carry a citrine stone or anoint yourself with any essential oil that smells empowering to you.

Raven Digitalis

May 10
Sunday

3rd ♒

Color of the day: Yellow
Incense of the day: Hyacinth

Mother's Day

A Mother's hands

I was with my mother when her spirit passed into Summerland. After she died, I sat quietly with her, holding her hands. And that's the first time I really noticed her hands. I marveled at all the love, work, and magic that came from those delicate hands. They prepared birthday cakes and wrapped beautiful gifts—just for me—and they wiped away my tears as a child.

This Mother's Day, magically honor your mother's hands. Don't wait like I did to appreciate your mother's hands. Find a photo of your mother holding you, and place it on your altar. Repay the work your mother's hands have done for you by creating something with your hands for her. You could prepare a meal, make a craft, or plant a pot of flowers yourself. As you do, see your mother's hands guiding you. Her hands will always be a part of you.

James Kambos

May 11
Monday

3rd ♒

☽ v/c 6:36 am
4th Quarter 6:36 am
☽ → ♓ 10:53 pm

Color of the day: Silver
Incense of the day: Narcissus

Illuminating Knowledge from the Past

There are few things more universally loved by esoteric folks than old books. We love books in general, but there is something magickal about old tomes. On this day back in the year 868 AD, a copy of the *Diamond Sutra* was printed in China, effectively making it the oldest known dated printed book.

Today, pull out a few of your oldest tomes. Try to find ones copywritten or printed before your birth. Contemplate the reasons you have them, and how their content and teachings are important to you. Light a candle invoking the illumination of knowledge, then envision its light surrounding you, enveloping you and the volume before you. Now read a favorite passage that has importance to you from the book, and absorb its wisdom and teaching as you bask in the light of illumination. So mote it be!

Blake Octavian Blair

May 12
Tuesday

4ħ ♓

Color of the day: White
Incense of the day: Ylang-ylang

Save the Turtles

Turtles are one of my totem animals and are creatures that I truly love. However, you can easily adapt this spell for other animals. Fill a chalice or goblet with water—preferably use ocean water, but spring water with salt added will work. By the light of a silver candle, charge three blue stones or glass marbles with energy to keep the turtles safe, and then drop them one by one into the chalice. I also like to put a small statue or image of a turtle near the chalice, although you could just write the animal's name on a piece of paper and tuck it under the chalice. Allow the candle to burn some each day—a half hour will work just fine. A pillar candle would be good for this spell, since it will burn longer before needing to be replaced.

Laurel Reufner

May 13
Wednesday

4ħ ♓
☽ v/c 12:55 pm

Color of the day: Topaz
Incense of the day: Lavender

Tarot Chaos Magick

This is a very simple act of chaos magick drawing on the energy of random synchronicity. Simply get a pack of inexpensive tarot cards. You may choose instead to smudge an old deck that you no longer use by burning sage.

In a quiet outdoor environment, enter a state of meditation while you shuffle the cards over and over again, with the intention of having each card becoming distributed to people who need the magick. While sitting, begin rocking back and forth. With each inhalation, raise up your head and breathe in the universal life force. With each exhalation, breathe the synchronistic chaos of the universe into the pack. Declare:

I affirm that each card will go to its intended recipient, to better their lives and provide insight amidst the chaos!

For the weeks and months that follow, proceed to covertly leave tarot cards in random public places, such as on a park bench, on the bus, on windshields, in grocery stores, and so on. Trust in the fact that each card will reach the person it's meant for and will provide them with some sort of much-needed insight.

Raven Digitalis

NOTES:

May 14
Thursday

4th ♓

☽ → ♈ 1:13 am

Color of the day: Turquoise
Incense of the day: Mulberry

Waning Moon in Waning Taurus

The Flower Moon is waning, and we're counting down to the end of the astrological sign of Taurus. Chances are excellent that no matter where you live, the weather this time of year is just about as perfect as it can be. Not too hot and not too cold, probably sunshine with a nice breeze. Consult almanacs and other research materials to discover your plant hardiness zone, if you do not already know it. Contribute to your compost heap with either spring or fall clean-up materials from the yards and gardens. If you have planted, a waning moon is the time to thin the plants. If the harvest is over, it is time to turn the soil. If you want to retard or control growth, or encourage hardy rooting, perform the necessary activities during the waning moon. Say:

Demeter and Persephone, guide me as the moon shines less each day. Help me tend the parcel of earth in my care.

Emyme

May 15
Friday

4th ♈

☽ v/c 8:04 am

Color of the day: Purple
Incense of the day: Orchid

Bittersweet Wisdom

Today is Chocolate Chip Day. It's easy to overlook the value of chocolate as something other than a tasty treat. It is sweet and delicious, but also dark and complex. This is the food of the gods, which humans can also enjoy.

Cocoa is actually an entheogen, known for raising human consciousness and connecting with the divine. It originated in Mesoamerica; its use dates back thousands of years. Chocolata is a modern personification of the chocolate goddess, often rendered as a Mesoamerican woman holding a cocoa plant or candy. She represents the bittersweet nature of life and knowledge.

Honor Chocolata by baking chocolate chip cookies. As the fragrance fills your home, concentrate on the spiritual importance of food. It is both pleasure and sustenance. Then eat mindfully. Knowledge can make us happy or sad, depending on what we do with it. This is the wisdom of chocolate and the inner divinity.

Elizabeth Barrette

May 16
Saturday

4th ♈

☽ → ♉ 3:02 am

Color of the day: Black
Incense of the day: Sage

Travel Talisman

Create a bundle for a safe journey by combining any of the following dried herbs and flowers in a white or red drawstring bag: rose petals, lilac (flowers or a piece of the branch), foxglove, devil's shoestring, wormwood, orris root, and witch hazel. Place a moonstone or piece of turquoise in the pouch with the herbs. Visualize a safe and pleasant journey and a joyful return home as you tie the pouch closed with a ribbon or string, making five knots. Repeat the following chant each time you tie the string:

As I wander, as I roam,

Far away or close to home;

Keep me safe along the way,

Guard my journey night and day.

Keep the bundle in your automobile or carry it with you while traveling.

Ember Grant

May 17

Sunday

♃ ♉

Color of the day: Orange
Incense of the day: Almond

Music Is My Mantra

Turning on the radio is something I do almost automatically as soon as I sit down at my desk or in the car. I've also come to learn that the universe has multiple ways of sending messages, whether it's tossing a coin in my path or hearing a song that plucks at my psyche.

Focus on your feelings today—is there anything you want to know, any questions you need answered? Turn on your favorite music service, and open yourself to the pieces being played. Does one song stick in your head? Is it the tune, or the words? Repeat them to yourself, or hum or sing them aloud.

Repeat the melody or the lyrics as a mantra whenever you feel you need them throughout the day. In your magical journal, write down the words, how they make you feel, and how they helped you.

Natalie Zaman

 May 18

Monday

♃ ♉

🌑 **New Moon 12:13 am**
☽ v/c 12:13 am
☽ → ♊ 5:27 am

Color of the day: Lavender
Incense of the day: Clary sage

New Moon of Fertile Earth

Though many Witches see winter as the season of earth, and spring as more attuned to the air element, the new moon in Taurus is a wonderful time to connect to earth in her active, fertile aspect and use this energy for growth and prosperity.

Obtain a potted thyme plant or some dried thyme. While touching the plant (or holding some of the dried herb), go into meditation. When you feel centered, visualize the sun, moon, and earth in perfect alignment, but instead of an eclipse, see silver/gold light shining down from the sun and moon to reach the earth beneath you. See this light merging with green light coming up from the earth, then see the gold, silver, and green lights fuse together, charging the herb and filling it with the power of spring and growth. The thyme can now be used to boost all magic for prosperity, growth, or healing.

Michael Furie

May 19
Tuesday

1st ♊

☽ v/c 1:57 pm

Color of the day: Maroon
Incense of the day: Cinnamon

Appalachian Well Magic

Wells are magical places because they serve as portals to the earth and they are dark and mysterious. Various forms of well magic are very popular in Appalachia. Wells are used for divination and for making wishes. For some reason, however, the belief exists that well magic is strongest if performed in May.

This spell will help you make a wish. Go to a well and pick up a stone that appeals to you. Breathe your intent into it, or whisper your wish to it. Carry the stone around the well three times, then throw it into the well. If your wish doesn't manifest in one month, try it again, preferably at a new moon.

James Kambos

May 20
Wednesday

1st ♊

☽ → ♋ 9:56 am

Color of the day: White
Incense of the day: Bay laurel

Wandcraft

The wand is a simple magickal tool to make at home. It need not be flawless, and it needs no wires, crystals, or bedazzling. Choose a natural branch spanning the length between your elbow and your extended fingers. If possible, allow the branch to dry for two to three weeks. Use a pocketknife to strip the bark and smooth any knots, then sand with several grades of sandpaper, beginning with coarse and working through fine grades until your wand is satiny smooth. Shape the end to a smooth round. Inscribe runes or designs with a woodburner, then rub with beeswax to seal and polish. Wrap in a fine, soft cloth. For women, charge by leaving the wand under the moon for a full month's cycle; for men, charge under the midday sun. Name your new wand, and keep it next to you until the two of you have come to know each other.

Susan Pesznecker

May 21
Thursday

1st ♋

☉ → ♊ 4:45 am

☽ v/c 8:36 pm

Color of the day: Purple
Incense of the day: Balsam

World Day for Cultural Diversity for Dialogue and Development

In November of 2001, in the wake of the terrorist attacks on 9/11, the United Nations sanctioned this day as a national holiday. The cultural diversity of earth-based belief systems continues to be misunderstood. Gather as many symbols of peace as you can find in your home. You may wish to go through magazines for pictures that symbolize peace to you. Place these on your altar for the day to give off power for your evening casting. If possible and appropriate, develop a valuable and harmonious dialogue with open and sympathetic followers of another religion. Educate one another. Look into opportunities for learning about other religions at a local library or college. At the evening casting, create a two- or three-dimensional representation of your idea of world peace. Bless and cleanse it with sea salt and sage. Display this in your home as a constant reminder to maintain an open mind and heart.

Emyme

May 22
Friday

1st ♋

☽ → ♌ 5:42 pm

Color of the day: Coral
Incense of the day: Mint

Harvey Milk

On this date in 1930, Harvey Milk was born. The first openly gay politician, Harvey Milk advocated for human rights and insisted that coming out of the closet would help heal the breach. Sadly, he was assassinated in 1978. As an iconic force for positive change, Harvey Milk lives on as a modern-day saint or archetypal ascended master who promotes self-acceptance, courage, and activism.

Today, create an altar to Harvey and ask for his help in speaking and living your truth and affecting positive change in the world. Consider his life story and all that he accomplished by being himself. Then, say an invocation, such as:

Harvey Milk, thank you for living bravely and providing such a positive example of courage and activism. Please help me to live as bravely and as fully as you did, and to create positive change within me and around me. Thank you.

Tess Whitehurst

May 23
Saturday

1st ♐ ♌

Color of the day: Blue
Incense of the day: Ivy

Rosalia

In classical Rome, today was the Rosalia, a festival celebrating goddesses of love. Venus was not always the great sex goddess. In early Rome, she was a domestic goddess who brought happiness to husbands and wives. She ruled kitchen gardens and happy homes long before she sponsored orgies and the romances of kings and queens. Celebrate the Rosalia today with an old-fashioned spell to find out who your next loved one might be.

Gather three rose petals or leaves, and assign the name of a potential love candidate to each one. Write their names on the petals with rose essential oil. As you do this, think about a possible future with each person. Promise unconditional love and friendship to all three. Set the named petals on your altar near a pink candle, light the candle, and invoke Venus. It's said that the rose petal that lasts the longest names your mate.

Barbara Ardinger, PhD

May 24
Sunday

1st ♐ ♌

☽ v/c 6:50 am

Color of the day: Amber
Incense of the day: Eucalyptus

Family harmony

Sunday is always a good day for family harmony. With all the stress of work, school, and the world you live in, you need some time together to bring peace and harmony to your family group. Making time for your family is the most important part of maintaining good family relationships.

It is not always easy to get everyone together, so planning in advance is always a good idea. And the best place to bring a family together is around the dinner table. At least once a month, make it a date for everyone to get together on a Sunday afternoon for a meal. Clear your calendar and let nothing interfere with that date.

And no matter what the weather, be sure to include some play. Nothing says harmony like a good meal and fun. Be sure to involve the whole family in the meal preparation and in planning the fun.

Boudica

May 25
Monday

1st ♉ ♌
☽ → ♍ 4:52 am
2nd Quarter 1:19 pm

Color of the day: White
Incense of the day: Rosemary

Memorial Day (observed)

Offerings to Mars

R egardless of how you may feel about the ongoing wars we are beset with currently, do your best to respect all of the lives lost in battle and to decorate the honorable dead with bravery and purpose.

If you feel called to, take time today to praise the mighty Mars, god of warfare, honor, and courage. Construct a shrine to Mars using an image or idol as the centerpiece. Around the altar, place any licensed guns (unarmed) and all household knives at the feet of the god of war. Take special care that the blades are pointing outward from Mars to invoke his strength, power, and protection. Offer rusty nails to be foundered by Mars into more useful technology.

Offer written prayers to give thanks and honor to those devotees of Mars who have lost their lives during this grave time of global conflict. If you have lost anyone personally in a war, place a candle for them, photos, and military identification tags near to Mars. As you do so, plead with the god of sacrifice to guide all armed forces and military officers through the land of the dead with peace and honor. Let the altar stand for the day.

Estha McNevin

NOTES:

May 26
Tuesday

2nd ♏

☽ v/c 10:21 pm

Color of the day: Gray
Incense of the day: Basil

Let Your Spiritual Power Sing!

On this date in 1939, Grammy and Tony Award–winning Canadian opera singer Teresa Stratas was born. Music is a wonderful method of raising energy and weaving magick, and you need not be an award-winning artist to do so. We all are capable of creating magick with our voices.

Today, vocalize aloud a favorite song or chant that inspires you spiritually, or even write your own! This is an act of magick in itself, as the spiritually relevant words voiced aloud are heard by the universe as a reaffirmation of your beliefs, intentions, and goals. This magickal exercise will also help you think about the power of the words you speak and of the music you listen to. If you have any additional magickal work you plan on doing today, a great energetic time and space to do so is after singing or chanting. Let your spiritual power sing!

Blake Octavian Blair

May 27
Wednesday

2nd ♏

☽ → ♎ 5:42 pm

Color of the day: Yellow
Incense of the day: Marjoram

Yes, No, Maybe So…

Stuck on a decision you need to make? Maybe you could use some outside input. Break out your deck of tarot cards (or a regular deck of cards and a means of interpreting them). Take a moment to figure out the phrasing of your question, keeping it as simple as possible. By the light of a candle, ground yourself enough to focus only on that question. With it in mind, shuffle the cards and deal out three across. As you lay out the cards, tell yourself "Yes," "No," and "Maybe I should think on it longer," Now you only need to interpret the cards, and you'll have their suggested answer. Usually the strongest positive card will be the correct one.

Laurel Reufner

May 28
Thursday

2nd ♎

Color of the day: Green
Incense of the day: Carnation

Air Elemental Spell

With Mercury in retrograde, intuition and instinct work better than words or phrases. Take a moment under this waxing moon to meditate on the energies of air. See beautiful cloud formations in your mind. Feel the lightness and purity of thought and intellect in the ethers around you. Feel and know the truth of the saying "Ideas are in the air." Smell and breathe the sweetness of the spring flowers all around you, and fill your lungs with the dawn breezes. Hear the wind chimes and the buzzing of hummingbirds, the caws of ravens and the sweet twitter and coo of other feathered creatures. Breathe deeply, filling your lungs all the way down to your toes.

Cast a circle in your mind, and vow to honor your breath and your ideas today, to nurture health, and pleasure, and rest. Promise to give your mind this honor from this day forward. Be blessed.

Thuri Calafia

May 29
Friday

2nd ♎
☽ v/c 4:20 pm

Color of the day: Pink
Incense of the day: Thyme

A Rampart of Protection

To increase the protective energy around you, situate yourself in a hexagram of candles by doing the following. In a dark, quiet area, take six tealight candles and put them equidistant apart, with you in the center. Stand with your hands outstretched to the cosmos, and draw down the limitless energy of the universe. Visualize this light filling your body and mind, and see the energy of the candles linking into the shape of a hexagram.

Chant *As above, so below* over and over again while you feel this flood of energy rushing into you and all around you. Finish by saying a prayer to the spirits, such as the following:

Holy guides, gods, and guardians, I ask you to surround me in a rampart of protection. Keep the maleficent far away from me. Illuminate my consciousness to see the proper path before me. In return, I shall humbly serve the force of the greater good. So mote it be!

Raven Digitalis

May 30

Saturday

2nd ♎

☽ → ♏ 5:34 am

Color of the day: Brown
Incense of the day: Sandalwood

Ganesha Mudra

Ganesha is a Hindu god portrayed with the head of an elephant. He is the remover of obstacles. He can also place obstacles to prevent undesirable things from happening. He is a patron of arts and sciences, balancing intellect with wisdom.

For the Ganesha mudra, place your left hand against your chest (horizontally), palm out. Overlap with your right hand, back of the hand facing out. Clasp hands, folding your fingers around each other. Without letting go, pull your hands outward, creating tension, and then release. Repeat several times. Then switch hands so that your left is back out and your right is palm out, going through the motions again. Finally, rest your hands softly over your heart. Meditate on feelings of peace.

This mudra symbolizes strength in the face of challenges. It warms and widens the heart. It helps you feel courageous and confident, making it easier to open up to other people.

Elizabeth Barrette

 May 31

Sunday

2nd ♏

Color of the day: Yellow
Incense of the day: Frankincense

A Forgiveness Stone

Forgiveness has more to do with you than the person you forgive. Alexander Pope said it well: "To err is human; to forgive, divine." To start the process, make a forgiveness stone.

Find a stone big enough to fill your hand. Holding it, think about the wrong done to you, the person who committed it, and all the details and feelings associated with it. Write everything on the stone in chalk, and visualize the stone absorbing all of it like a sponge. Take the stone to a place of running water. Meditate on it one last time, then throw it into the water, with these words:

We've been together long enough,

And now I set you free.

The forgiveness that I give to you

Is freedom, too, for me.

The water will wash away any lingering negativity. Knowing this, turn and walk away.

Natalie Zaman

June

The month of June is named for Juno, the principal goddess of the Roman pantheon and wife of Jupiter. She is the patroness of marriage and the well-being of women. This is one reason June is the most popular month for weddings. June brings the magic of Midsummer—the summer solstice, the longest day of the year. Summer is ripe now with bird song and the pleasant buzz of evening insects. The gentleness of spring has given way to the powerful heat of summer—the full moon of June is called the Strong Sun Moon. Various cultures pay homage to sun gods this time of year. In some places summer is just getting started and the hottest months are yet to come, yet after the solstice we don't even notice the days beginning to get slightly shorter. This is the time for enjoying the splendor of summer: playful picnics and hikes through the woods, long nights beneath the stars, tending gardens and flower beds. Roadsides are a riot of color, and herbs such as St. John's wort, vervain, and yarrow can be used in herbal amulets. This is the time of year to honor the faeries—leave offerings for them of ale, milk, fruit, or bread before cutting flowers or herbs, and they may help your garden grow.

Ember Grant

June 1
Monday

2nd ♏

☽ v/c 7:01 am

☽ → ♐ 2:39 pm

Color of the day: Silver

Incense of the day: Lily

Out with the Old and in with the New!

Today marks Koromo-Gaye, the Japanese clothes-changing festival. Today Japanese people put away their heavier winter clothing and bring out and begin wearing lighter summer weight and colored garb. Aside from the practical aspect, this event has deep ritual significance and is often carried out regardless of climate.

Today, in the spirit of "out with the old and in with the new," think of something, wardrobe or otherwise, that isn't currently functionally serving you. Pack it away until such time that it will be of functional use again, or if you won't need the item in the future, pass it along to someone it will be of use to. Now, if you have something of which you have been in need, you have made both the physical and energetic space for it, so look into its acquisition. Afterward, declare:

Out with the old and in with the new,
blessed balance, I honor you!

Blake Octavian Blair

 # June 2
Tuesday

2nd ♐

🌕 Full Moon 12:19 pm

Color of the day: Scarlet

Incense of the day: Bayberry

June Moon Love Spell

Life's meaning begins and ends with love, and while June's full Strawberry Moon can certainly be romantic, it can also be a time to recharge your love for yourself. Remember how lovable you are with this ritual. You will need red rose petals and a ripe strawberry.

Stand under the full moon. Take a handful of rose petals (June's full moon is also known as Rose Moon) and, moving clockwise, scatter them in a circle around yourself. When the circle is complete, call out:

Love I deserve,

With no reserve,

From others and from me.

This I remember, blessed be!

Look at the strawberry and be aware of its heart shape. See it as the embodiment of love—and take a bite. Feel the prickle of the seeds on your tongue, and taste its sweetness. Know that you are surrounded by love and that it dwells inside you.

Natalie Zaman

June 3
Wednesday

3rd ♐

☽ v/c 1:59 am

☽ → ♑ 8:50 pm

Color of the day: White
Incense of the day: Lavender

Clover Spell for Communication

While the four-leaf clover is symbolic of good fortune, no matter how many leaves the clover has, it's useful in magic. Clover, in general, is associated with the god Mercury and the element of air. Since Wednesday is associated with Mercury, the Roman messenger god, today is a perfect day to use this plant in a spell to clear away mixed messages in your communication. Ask for the help of the four winds to clarify your words and expressions and improve your listening skills. Hold the clover and face each direction as you chant:

East, carry my words.

South, let them be clear.

West, let them be true.

North, may I think first.

East, help me to hear.

South, may I listen with care.

West, help me respond.

North, let me know when to speak.

Keep the clover where you can see it, remembering that listening is a vital part of communication.

Ember Grant

NOTES:

June 4
Thursday

3rd ♑

Color of the day: Purple
Incense of the day: Jasmine

Casting Out Bad Luck

There are times when you mis-speak and worry that you are inviting trouble. Or maybe you accidentally break a mirror and want to ward off any bad luck that could generate. A quick way to remove any bad luck is to pick up a stone on the ground with your strong hand. Visualize any bad luck you may have around you as a dark haze, then mentally send it down into the stone, where it will stay.

To be rid of the bad luck perma-nently, throw the stone as hard as you can away from you, preferably into a moving body of water, though this isn't totally necessary. Just throw it far away and leave the area, being careful not to look back.

Michael Furie

June 5
Friday

3rd ♑
☽ v/c 6:54 am

Color of the day: Rose
Incense of the day: Yarrow

A Bride and Groom Spell

This spell should be performed by the bride and groom together two or three days before the wedding. Use this spell to ensure a strong, happy union.

You'll need two red candles, some gold ribbon, two red roses in a clear vase, and a pretty box that will hold the candles. Place the roses in the center of your altar, with the candles on either side. The bride should light one candle first, then the groom will light the other one. Now slowly push the candles together until almost touching. Visualize your union growing stron-ger. Together, when you feel it's the right moment, say:

Fire bright, fire spark,

Our hearts shall never part.

Snuff out the candles. When the candles are cool, tie them together with the gold ribbon. Then place them in the box. You may repeat this spell on your first anniversary.

James Kambos

June 6
Saturday

3rd ♑

☽ → ♒ 1:02 am

Color of the day: Gray
Incense of the day: Rue

Christening New Garden Clogs

For this spell, assemble:

+ One new pair of garden clogs

+ Sea salt water for cleansing

+ Patchouli oil for anointing

+ Four cups birdseed

+ A towel for drying

Carefully wash the clogs in sea salt water, and encourage any negative, lazy, or unlucky energy to depart from them. Gently dry them with a clean towel. Next, anoint the top, bottom, toe, heel, and either side of each clean clog with patchouli oil to bless them as vehicles of wealth and growth. Finally, fill each clog completely with birdseed, and leave them in the garden overnight to be blessed by the fairies and creatures of Mother Nature. The next morning, scatter the seed along the garden paths to ensure graceful gardening and a fruitful path ahead.

Estha McNevin

June 7
Sunday

3rd ♒

☽ v/c 10:30 am

Color of the day: Amber
Incense of the day: Frankincense

Spell for Justice

Sometimes we find ourselves in a dispute that requires litigation. Tarot cards can be used in spell workings to signify intent and assist in focusing on the outcome we desire.

Justice is a great card in disputes. A judge balances his or her decision with morality, duty, and rights. The judge's decision will be based on the facts. Remember, not every claim can be met, but you can look to the balance of the dispute coming out in your favor. Add the High Priestess card, she who discovers hidden knowledge; look to uncovering the truth.

The association of Athena with Justice can give us the divine push we need. It was Athena who is credited with establishing justice as more than a heavy hand dealing out punishment. She is credited with putting aside vengeance for fairness. Ask her for that fairness in your cause.

Boudica

June 8
Monday

3rd ♒
☽ → ♓ 4:16 am

Color of the day: Lavender
Incense of the day: Hyssop

Fire Elemental Spell

With Mercury in retrograde, intuition and instinct work better than words or phrases. Take a moment under this waning moon to meditate on the energies of fire, both its ability to warm and to deconstruct. See blazing peaks of flames in your mind, and feel the warmth and the potential for destruction swirling around you. Know that this is the path of passion—whether political or spiritual, emotional or sexual, passion can be incredibly creative or devastatingly destructive. Think about all the things you feel passionately about, and allow that energy to rise up and fill your entire being. Focus your attention on simply feeling that energy for a while, without judgment. Allow yourself to know the truth that passion in and of itself is neither right nor wrong, but it's what we do with it that makes it so. Breathe deeply, opening to the warmth, the fire, the blazing heat of your passion, and promise yourself that you will honor your passions by being true to them from this day forward. Blessed be.

Thuri Calafia

June 9
Tuesday

3rd ♓
4th Quarter 11:42 am
☽ v/c 2:08 pm

Color of the day: White
Incense of the day: Ylang-ylang

Living Air

The air element is associated with inspiration, intellect, and creativity, for air is dynamic and always moving in ways that cannot be predicted or anticipated. The air element is manifest by ideas, motivation, dreams, wishes, and travel.

Spend a day (or longer) focusing deeply on your connection to the air element. Dress in light cottons and linens in soft blue, white, and other airy pastel colors, and add a gauzy scarf to move with the breeze. Carry adventurine, sodalite, or ulexite—stones associated with air. Surround yourself with wind chimes, small paper windmills mounted on sticks, helium balloons, and spirit flags.

For an air-centered ritual, inscribe spells or manifestations on a kite, and send it into the air; feel the energy come back to you through the kite string. Send yourself skyward along the string, dancing through the air with your magickal kite!

Susan Pesznecker

June 10
Wednesday

4th ♓
☽ → ♈ 7:14 am

Color of the day: Brown
Incense of the day: Bay laurel

Align with Time

Japanese Crown Prince Tenchi (emperor from approximately 663 to 671) adored his water clock, and on this date proclaimed that bells and drums must mark the hours. In 1920, today became Japan's *Toki no Kinenbi*, or Time Observance Day, a celebration of punctuality during which watchmakers provide free repairs. Capitalize on the energy generated by this nationwide observance with a ritual to align you harmoniously with time, something that reaps many benefits. Feeling that you have an abundance of time, for example (rather than rushing around madly from activity to activity), can instill you with a sense of serenity and self-mastery. First, make sure that all your clocks are accurate and in working order. Then anoint each one lightly with frankincense essential oil (or just bless each one by visualizing it filled with light) as you affirm:

I am harmoniously aligned with time.

I have an abundance of time.

Time is on my side.

Tess Whitehurst

 June 11
Thursday

4th ♈
☽ v/c 7:43 pm

Color of the day: White
Incense of the day: Myrrh

Balance head and heart

Some of us are too "thoughty," and others are too "feelie." The ideal is to balance head and heart. We cannot truly thrive if we lack either intellect or emotions.

Online or in a book, find the symbols of the fourth (heart) and sixth (brow) chakras. As you study these two chakras and learn their meanings, find a way to create the symbols. Embroider them, fashion them with wire, or draw them. As you create these two symbols, feel the powers of the chakras flowing through your fingers, up your arms, and into your body. Let the energy of each symbol settle in its proper place in your body. Hold the two symbols you've sewn or forged or drawn in your open hands, side by side, and visualize the energies coming into balance inside you. As you go about your day, keep the symbols nearby and hold their balanced energies in your consciousness.

Barbara Ardinger, PhD

June 12
Friday

4th ♈

☽ → ♉ 10:16 am

Color of the day: Pink
Incense of the day: Rose

Enchanting a Pendant Through Dance

Talismans and charms that are worn as jewelry can help connect us to the other worlds and provide an extra layer of metaphysical protection throughout the day. This working can be used for a necklace pendant, ring, earring, or pocket charm.

Put a special pendant of your choice on a table in a relatively empty room or ritual space. Be sure that all lights are out, save for a candle and incense in the center. Strip skyclad (nude) and begin walking in a deosil (clockwise) fashion around the table. Blur your vision and begin to clap in a rhythmic manner to help induce an altered state of consciousness. Dance and flail around in any way you are guided. While you are doing this, visualize the intentions you wish to place into the pendant.

As you work yourself into a state of consciousness that matches your purpose, quickly point your hands to the piece to project the energy into it. Do this on repeat, with a loud *HAH!* or similar noise to represent the projection of energy into the piece. Repeat this until you feel the item is fully enchanted.

Raven Digitalis

NOTES:

June 13
Saturday

4th ♉

☽ v/c 6:06 pm

Color of the day: Black
Incense of the day: Ivy

Sewing Machine Spell

Today is Sewing Machine Day. This device automated sewing so that people no longer had to make every garment by hand-stitching. Using a sewing machine used to be a ubiquitous skill, but has since dwindled. Some Pagans still make their own ritual robes with a sewing machine, or by hand, because they feel that instills more magic into the finished product.

There are many other small appliances that make our lives more convenient. Here is a spell to protect them and keep them running. You'll need a washer or any other tiny machine part. Hold it to the side of a new appliance to take an imprint of being in perfect working order. Then say:

Bright and new,

Stay so true,

Working for me,

So mote it be!

Concentrate on that smooth running. Keep the washer near your sewing machine or other appliances.

Elizabeth Barrette

June 14
Sunday

4th ♉

☽ → ♊ 1:51 pm

Color of the day: Gold
Incense of the day: Hyacinth

Flag Day

Sunday Spell for Banishment

According to Hebrew calendars, Sunday is considered the first day of the week. As we ease into a new week, let's take advantage of the waning moon and do a little banishment magick. Gather a small chime-size candle and appropriate holder and a toothpick, skewer, or other implement suitable for carving into the candle. Think of something in your life that you'd like to lessen or banish. Think of something that is no longer serving your highest good. Carve what you wish to banish into the side of the candle. Hold the candle between your hands and up to your third eye. Concentrate on your intent and project it into the candle. Place the candle in its holder and recite a simple incantation such as:

Fire, fire, burning bright,

Incinerate and banish under waning moon light.

Envision the light of the flame engulfing, banishing, and transmuting that which you intend to banish. So mote it be!

Blake Octavian Blair

June 15
Monday

4th ♊

Color of the day: Gray
Incense of the day: Neroli

A Good healthy Soak

Take time for your own good health and enjoy a nice relaxing bath. You can mix up this concoction and keep it handy near the tub.

Combine the following ingredients in a medium-size glass bowl. As you add each herb, charge it with its particular intention. Use four parts rose petals (love), two parts carnation petals (strength), two parts lavender (peace), two parts lemon peel (courage), and one part dried, grated ginger (healing). Stir together well and store in a sealed, dry container.

To use, place ½ cup of the mix in a small muslin bag and toss into the running water along with ½ cup Epsom salt. If you don't have any muslin bags, place the bath mix in the middle of a washcloth and fasten it with a rubber band or some string. Make sure to use a cloth that you don't mind staining.

Laurel Reufner

June 16
Tuesday

4th ♊
☽ v/c 10:05 am
New Moon 10:05 am
☽ → ♋ 6:51 pm

Color of the day: Red
Incense of the day: Geranium

A New Moon Love Spell

A new moon in June is an auspicious time to begin a love spell, and many June flowers are excellent to use if you wish to attract love. For this spell, we'll make a love-attracting sachet. Begin this spell just before sunset. You'll need a leaf from lady's mantle, a leaf and some flowers from a red geranium, and some red rose petals.

Once you have your plant materials, place them in the center of a square piece of red fabric. Focus on your intent as you tie the corners of the fabric together with white ribbon. At dark, go outside and hold your sachet toward the sky as you say:

With these herbs of three,

Send love to me.

Hide your sachet until the full moon. Then sprinkle the contents of your sachet on the ground beneath the full moon as an offering.

James Kambos

June 17
Wednesday

1st ♋

Color of the day: Topaz
Incense of the day: Honeysuckle

Tissue Butterfly Divination

Cut thirty-three butterfly shapes out of different-colored tissue papers, or purchase tissue confetti in butterfly shapes and count out thirty-three. On each one, write a potential answer to the divination question at hand. Do your best to make up new and extreme outcomes to your question. Finally, collect them all and take them to the highest location in your house. Ask the following question:

> Will the butterfly before my eye reveal to me a truth or a lie?

Next, go to other areas of the house where you contemplate this outcome and ask the question again. Finally, go outside and release the butterflies into an uplifted gust of wind. Any that stay will reveal your answer.

Estha McNevin

NOTES:

June 18
Thursday

1st ♋

Color of the day: Crimson
Incense of the day: Clove

Respite from the World

Everyone needs to get away once in a while and be solitary. Everyone needs to take time and just be still—to just BE. If you are a primary caregiver, a weekend away every few months is a healthy respite. Take these opportunities and collect items for remembrance bags or memory jars. Pack self-seal plastic bags of various sizes, small lidded jars, and square scraps of fabric. Be on the lookout for found items that hold special meaning. A trip to the sea or lake may yield a pretty shell or tumbled glass, some sand, or a small piece of driftwood. Look for unusual stones, flowers, or leaves along a hiking path. Receipts, a bit of earth, business cards…any little bit may be the right ingredient.

On a recent trip to a rural area, I discovered five feathers by my car. Another trip yielded a tiny pine cone out of a bowl of potpourri in my room. (Be careful not to plunder—that would bring bad energy.)

Using your travel altar kit, cleanse and bless the items. With intention, place them in the jar or plastic bag, or gather the fabric into a pouch with ribbon. Take advantage of the solitude to spark your creative fire and write out a spell. Be sure to identify the contents and the date with a decorative label or tag. Hang up your item as a reminder of your trip, or store in a cool, dark space where the contents will quietly give off their power. After a few years, bury the item.

Emyme

NOTES:

June 19
Friday

1st ♋

☽ v/c 1:52 am

☽ → ♌ 2:23 am

Color of the day: White
Incense of the day: Violet

Luck Be a Ladybug

Ladybugs are symbols of luck in many cultures and are also helpful in keeping harmful insects at bay. Welcome ladybug energy into your life and garden tonight after sunset. (This will allow the magic to incubate overnight. It is also a good time to release ladybugs; darkness and coolness are ideal environmental conditions for them to get acclimated to a new area.) And how lucky that the moon is waxing—good for growth! You'll need a container of ladybugs, which can be ordered online or purchased at a garden center.

Bring your ladybugs into your garden. Lay the container on the ground near plants, remove the lid, and speak this invocation:

Dearest winged lady friend,

I share my home with thee.

Fly away, return again,

Bless my garden and bless me!

Watch your garden and your good fortune grow!

Natalie Zaman

 June 20
Saturday

1st ♌

Color of the day: Blue
Incense of the day: Patchouli

Spell to Promote Clear Communication

Slippery elm is an herb that is widely known to stop gossip. It does not do this in a malicious way, however; it is a calming herb. Slippery elm can be used to soothe misunderstandings between people who fail to communicate properly. To help someone understand what you are trying to say, write down exactly what you mean on a piece of paper, preferably in yellow or orange ink (or the paper can be yellow or orange), and light some slippery elm on an incense charcoal in your cauldron.

Light a yellow candle charged with the desire to truly communicate, and use it to burn the paper. Drop the paper into the cauldron, and speak what you are trying to communicate out loud as if the person was standing in front of you. Extinguish the candle and incense. When they have cooled, bury the remains. The person should become more understanding.

Michel Furie

June 21
Sunday

1st ♈ ♌

☽ v/c 12:09 pm

☉ → ♋ 12:38 pm

☽ → ♍ 12:59 pm

Color of the day: Yellow
Incense of the day: Heliotrope

Litha – Summer Solstice – Father's Day

A Solitary Midsummer Celebration

Put together a small lunch consisting of a fresh leafy green salad, some strawberries, and some fruit juice, and take along a journal or writing paper and a writing instrument. Find a grassy spot and settle down to enjoy some quality time with Mother Gaia.

The magical part of this ritual will focus on bringing abundance into your life. The greens in the salad represent the intent for this working, and as you eat, you take into yourself the abundance of the earth at this time of year, and all it means for personal growth. The strawberries, fresh and abundant in the summer, represent the sweetness and ripeness of the world that we live in and our ability to pick our successes when they are rich and ready to be enjoyed. You are absorbing the magic into yourself as you eat, to be used to make your life more affluent and successful.

Think about where you want to go in the next few months. Write down your thoughts as you eat, and contemplate your next projects. Finish off with some fresh fruit juice, being sure to offer some of it as a libation to your gods/goddesses for future successful projects.

Boudica

NOTES:

June 22
Monday

1st ♍

Color of the day: White
Incense of the day: Lily

hag Stone Charging Spell

Used traditionally for protection and good fortune and to increase vitality, holey stones, or "hag" stones, have naturally occurring holes through them—often the result of exposure to running water or other natural types of erosion. Since we're near the height of summer, and the moon is waxing, now is a good time to charge this special stone for the purpose of your choice. Choose a place outside where you can keep this stone (even a potted plant will work), and allow it to remain there for a day or two, even several months, exposing it to rain, sunlight, and moonlight—a powerful combination of the earth and water elements. Chant:

Fortune, healing, and protection,
Secrets guard beyond detection.
Honored place in my collection,
Guide me in the right direction.

Ember Grant

June 23
Tuesday

1st ♍

Color of the day: Black
Incense of the day: Ginger

Weeding Your Garden

We've just passed the summer solstice, which according to the astronomers is the beginning of summer but to those of us who really know is Midsummer, the high point (and hinge) of the season. Although the weather is likely to get hotter, we're on the downhill side of summer and the solstice energy is waning. This is a good time for cleaning and clearing.

Whether you have a real (outdoor) garden or a large or small collection of potted plants, visit your garden today and clean it up. Find the uninvited guests—weeds or bugs—and uproot them and send them far away. As you're working, also consider your internal garden. What's growing in your mind? In your heart? Find the weeds inside you and pull them up by the roots. Find the infestations and banish them. Complete this work by stating an intention to bloom with kindness and intelligence.

Barbara Ardinger, PhD

June 24
Wednesday

1st ♍

☽ v/c 1:12 am

☽ → ♎ 1:41 am

2nd Quarter 7:03 am

Color of the day: Yellow
Incense of the day: Lilac

Good Luck Spell

Today is a day to celebrate and honor Lady Luck, according to Z Budapest in *The Grandmother of Time*. For this spell, you'll need three candles for the three Fates: Clotho, who spins the threads of fate; Lachesis, who measures the thread and thereby determines how long our lives will be; and Atropos, who cuts the threads of life when our time to cross over has come. Governed by eternal laws, the major aspects of the weavings of the Fates (such as our lifespans) cannot be changed, but our luck can be improved!

Choose candles in a color having to do with the energies of the luck you wish to change. Light the first candle and say:

Clotho, spinner of the threads of fate, please send beneficial luck my way.

Light the second candle and say:

Lachesis, measurer of the lives of mortals, please send luck for the remainder of my journey here on this earth.

Light the third candle and say:

Atropos, cutter of the threads, I thank you for the time I have been allotted here, but please help me to improve the quality of my life.

Then bless them all and thank them all. Let the candles burn down as your offering to these powerful goddesses.

Thuri Calafia

NOTES:

June 25
Thursday

2nd ♎

☽ v/c 7:22 pm

Color of the day: Green
Incense of the day: Nutmeg

Shower Blessing

Here is a simple ritual to start your day on a magickal note. As you step into the shower, dip your head under the water, saying:

May I be cleansed. May all anger, frustration, and negativity flow off of me as rain washes dust from the leaves.

Dip a second time and say:

May I be purified. May the waters of life anoint me as they did when I slipped new from my mother's womb.

Dip a third and final time, saying:

May I be strengthened. May the water's life-giving nature create for me a barrier of health and vigor that no ills may penetrate.

As you repeat the last part, envision the water cloaking you with protection. Step from the shower and towel off. With a quick *So mote it be*, step with confidence into your day.

Susan Pesznecker

June 26
Friday

2nd ♎

☽ → ♏ 1:57 pm

Color of the day: Purple
Incense of the day: Vanilla

Pay the Piper

In Germany, today is Pied Piper Day. Perhaps the Pied Piper's story is enduring because we all sense the power of unpaid debts to wreak havoc in other areas of our lives—not because of external forces punishing us, but because of an internal sense of fairness that may cause leaks in our energy and precipitate less-than-desirable conditions. Instead of letting it get to that point, pay the piper what he's owed. In a journal, brainstorm any literal or figurative areas where you feel indebted. For example, perhaps you never properly thanked someone for a favor, or perhaps you actually owe someone some cash. After brainstorming, choose one way you can move toward paying each debt back today. Even if you can't begin to repay the debt itself—for example, if you've lost contact with the person—pay the karmic debt by giving something similar to a charity or someone in need.

Tess Whitehurst

June 27
Saturday

2nd ♏

Color of the day: Brown
Incense of the day: Magnolia

Magickal Floor Wash

You can create a magickal floor wash, to be used on hard surfaces with a mop, by combining one part hydrogen peroxide, three parts vinegar, and six parts hot water. Add a few drops of organic essential oil and a pinch of sea salt. Shake up this mixture, and visualize the bottle surrounded in protective white and yellow light. Add a quartz crystal, amethyst, citrine, or other gemstone aligned with protection.

Before using the floor wash, let the bottle sit in the light of the moon and the sun for at least three days and nights. If you're able, assist the spell's energy by holding the bottle in front of the moon or sun whenever possible. Visualize the energy entering the bottle and providing a boost. Further enchant the bottle by speaking words into it each day.

When ready, use the floor wash as a mopping liquid or simply scatter it around your house. This versatile liquid may also be used in small quantities in the shower or bathtub.

Raven Digitalis

June 28
Sunday

2nd ♏

☽ v/c 9:50 pm
☽ → ♐ 11:21 pm

Color of the day: Orange
Incense of the day: Juniper

Burning with Passion

Passion applies to more than just romance. It also provides necessary energy for completing projects, especially creative ones. If you have an assignment for work or school that doesn't enthuse you, here is a spell to help generate excitement for it.

For this spell, you'll need a red candle in a holder and some hot paprika. Etch the candle with a word or symbol that represents your project. Sprinkle paprika in a triangle around the candle. Then light the wick and say:

Creature of fire,

Heat my desire.

With tool or toy,

Let work bring joy.

Meditate on the energy of fire and the nature of your project. Let the candle burn down in a safe place. If you need a reminder, keep a bit of the leftover wax to carry or incorporate into your project.

Elizabeth Barrette

June 29
Monday

2nd ♐

Color of the day: Lavender
Incense of the day: Narcissus

Celebration for San Pedro (Saint Peter)

Every year on this date, the town of Haro, Spain, celebrates with a wine festival in honor of the patron saint San Pedro. Celebrants wear white shirts and red scarves. The main event of the day is the Battle of Wine, in which everyone throws red wine at one another until the crowd is filled with pink shirts. After all are soaked, the day continues with food and (of course!) wine, and various contests and competitions.

Even if you are not a wine drinker, this is a good day to celebrate the good life. Place dark red and purple candles on your altar. Add a picture of your favorite god or goddess of the fruit of the vine. Wear a red scarf, tie, socks, or piece of jewelry. Include grapes or grape juice with your meals, and wine (or juice) with your cakes and ale after casting. Express gratitude for all the blessings of your life before you retire.

Emyme

June 30
Sunday

2nd ♐
☽ v/c 2:18 pm

Color of the day: Gray
Incense of the day: Cedar

Fairy Welcome

Apparently, many among the Fae like the rosemary plant. Attempt to draw them to your humble abode with this simple action. You'll need a rosemary plant, either planted in your garden or in a nice pot, and enough small white pebbles with which to ring the stem. Small dishes of milk and honey should be set off to the side of the pebbles—dishes from a child's tea set would work nicely. Replace the milk and honey often, and take good care of the rosemary plant to encourage the fairies to stick around.

Laurel Reufner

July

Oh, July… Sweet month of sun and flowers, the "Wednesday hump" of summer. In July, life is easy. The power of the Sun God is at its peak, and all is growing and flourishing, bursting from the earth as a gift of Beltane's fertility and heading inevitably toward the Mabon harvests as the Wheel makes its inexorable turns. In July, the flowers smell sweetest and the trees are the greenest as burgeoning life fuels our creativity and gifts us with long rapturous days, wild for the taking.

July is a wonderful time to care for your local faery folk. Create a small shrine for them in your yard or garden. Leave out a saucer with a bit of honey and butter—they will appreciate it, and may bless you with wisdom and joy. Keep some rue in your pocket to avoid being led astray by the faeries in one of their wilder moments!

You might also craft a protective summer herbal amulet. Gather either three or nine of the following herbs before sunrise: chamomile, clover, comfrey, ivy, lavender, mugwort, nettle, plantain, rose, rue, St. John's wort, sweet woodruff, thyme, wort, vervain, and yarrow. Dry the herbs in a cool, dark place for a few days, then crumble and use to fill a small pouch. Carry, wear, or keep your summer amulet nearby for blessings and protection.

Susan Pesznecker

July 1
Wednesday

2nd ♐

☽ → ♑ 5:11 am

Full Moon 10:20 pm

Color of the day: Topaz
Incense of the day: Lavender

Full Moon Knot Magick

Go to an area outside under the full moon where you will not be disturbed. With a durable three-foot white cord in hand, tie a series of nine knots. Pretend to "tie the moon" into each knot by holding the cord up to the moon, and, with one eye closed, see the knot roping the moon. Visualize each knot surrounded by the light of the moon. Perform any additional magick, meditation, or lunar observation at this time.

Because the full moon represents manifestations and wishes, save the cord for later use by placing it in an all-natural black bag. At any time in the future when you feel low on energy or feel the need to say a prayer or make a wish, simply untie a knot and "breathe in" the energy as you do so. Blow this energy back into the night-time air while you make the wish, weaving the energy from the illuminated past into the present moment.

Raven Digitalis

July 2
Thursday

3rd ♑

Color of the day: White
Incense of the day: Carnation

Assess Your Personal Plan

It is time to measure your personal growth by how far you have come this summer with your projects and goals and how much further you need to grow before you achieve those goals.

Take your journal and read back to where you set your personal goals for this year. Write down the ones you have been working on, and see how far you have progressed. This is the halfway mark, and you need to be constantly looking at how far you want to go, how far you have gone, and how much more you need to get there. If you didn't start a journal, then it's time you did.

Take your measures, and then set down your realistic goals for this year. Concentrate your efforts in the areas where you can succeed, and leave those projects that have not quite made the grade for next year.

Boudica

July 3
Friday

3rd ♑

☽ v/c 6:38 am

☽ → ♒ 8:21 am

Color of the day: Pink
Incense of the day: Cypress

A Confidence Spell

Tap into the sun's energy with this July spell to build your self-confidence. Light an orange or yellow pillar candle. Around the base of the candle, sprinkle some marigold petals and foliage. Sit before the candle, and relax and center yourself. Form a vision in your mind of whatever it is you wish to accomplish. Now open your eyes and gaze at the candle's flame. Watch as it grows, and really look at its colors—yellow, orange, and gold. See the colors mingling, glowing like a mini sun. See yourself in the center of the flame achieving your goal. Begin to chant:

I can, I will, I must!

Chant at least three times. After chanting, breathe deeply three times. Return to your everyday world. Extinguish the candle.

End the ritual by placing the marigold petals/foliage in a small dish, and keep on your altar to keep the spell active.

James Kambos

July 4
Saturday

3rd ♒

Color of the day: Black
Incense of the day: Sage

Independence Day

Declare Your Independence

Today is Independence Day in the United States, a day to celebrate and reassess our freedoms. What holds you captive? Declare your independence from whatever is holding you back with this tarot spell.

Lay down the Devil card. This is you now—full of potential, but chained under the Beast. Write that from which you would be freed on a piece of paper, and place it on top of the Devil.

Hold the Lovers card in your hand. This is where you want to be—blessed by the Divine and free to choose your own destiny. Speak aloud:

I declare my independence from [habit]. It holds no power over me.

Cover the Devil card and slip of paper with the Lovers card. Look at the Lovers when you need a boost in confidence. At the end of the day, burn the paper and blow the ashes into the wind.

Natalie Zaman

July 5
Sunday

3rd ♒

☽ v/c 8:32 am

☽ → ♓ 10:23 am

Color of the day: Yellow
Incense of the day: Marigold

Spell to Enchant a Child's Stuffed Animal

Here is a spell to help children who are afraid of the dark or of "monsters" under the bed. It acts to charge a favorite stuffed animal or chosen toy to become a protective amulet. The first time this is done, the parent can do this with a great deal of showmanship and then the child can reinforce the spell as needed.

Holding the chosen toy, and recite the following to charge it with power:

Stars above and magic moon,

Fill this toy with power.

Keep me (my child) safe the whole night through,

Each and every hour.

Several toys could be enchanted to act as wards and placed around the room if a stronger amount of protection is needed or desired.

Michael Furie

 July 6
Monday

3rd ♓

Color of the day: Lavender
Incense of the day: Clary sage

Wellness Brew

Infusing herbs and plants with water, like making tea, is a kind of "witch's brew." Today, focus on your well-being and finding balance in your life by creating a magical brew using your favorite tea. Begin by simply brewing yourself a cup. While your tea is steeping, hold your hands over the cup (be careful of the hot steam) and say the following words:

May this brew bring harmony

And balance to my life.

May this brew bring wellness, too,

In times of stress and strife.

When you're ready to drink your tea, imagine the water infused with the magic of the plants and flowers, and their energy filling you with a calm, balanced state of mind. Drink and be well. Repeat the spell as often as you like. Make this visualization part of your daily cup of tea.

Ember Grant

July 7
Tuesday

3rd ♓

☽ v/c 10:36 am

☽ → ♈ 12:38 pm

Color of the day: Red
Incense of the day: Cinnamon

Change Your Luck with Dollar Deliveries

For this spell, assemble the following items:

- Eleven individual one dollar bills

- Eleven thank-you cards

- Eleven quotes regarding success

In each card, write a different quote relating to success. These quotes should inspire you and be reminders of the potential that can sometimes go unnoticed when we focus more on money than the character it requires to truly earn it. Place a dollar bill inside each card, and seal it in an envelope. On the outside, address each envelope "For you."

Throughout the day, mysteriously leave your messages of prosperity in random locations where individuals will find them. Once you deliver a missive, walk away knowing that all good deeds are rewarded. Contemplate the unknown people who will receive your dollar bills. Let each delivery be an ambitious opportunity to change your luck.

Estha McNevin

NOTES:

July 8
Wednesday

3rd ♈
4th Quarter 4:24 pm

Color of the day: Brown
Incense of the day: Bay laurel

Spell of Discarding

Tonight's moon, a waning one in Aries, just as the sun has passed the solstice, is most auspicious for discarding and banishing negative energies. For this spell, you will need a fireproof dish, such as a small cauldron, plus a black candle and some gray paper. Take a moment to jot down all the energies you wish to discard, each on a small piece of the gray paper. Be sure to include all your "labels"—those things that others have said about you or that you have said about yourself that you do not agree with or no longer find to be true. Take your time and think deeply about these energies. Then, one by one, burn them in the candle flame and drop them into the cauldron, watching them burn away forever. Say:

As the moon dies, as the sun dies, as the year dies, so let these falsehoods about me die, never to return.

After the last one, say *So mote it be* with all the courage and conviction you can muster. Know that you are healed. And so mote it be.

Thuri Calafia

July 9
Thursday

4th ♈
☽ v/c 9:47 am
☽ → ♉ 3:49 pm

Color of the day: Green
Incense of the day: Apricot

Clear Limiting Beliefs about Money

As magical practitioners, our thoughts and beliefs are especially powerful, so we want to make sure they're all on our side. Today, do some inner excavation to get rid of old, limiting beliefs about money. Light a white candle and some clearing incense such as cedar or sage. Then, on a piece of paper, list any limiting beliefs about money that you can think of. Examples: "Money is hard to come by." "If it's not one thing, it's another." "Abundance is limited: the more I have, the less someone else has." "Rich people are snobs." In a new list, question each belief and jot down at least three ways that it isn't actually true, or isn't always true. Finally, make a third list: turn each belief around and formulate a new, more empowering one. Read it aloud with conviction. Safely burn the original list, and flush the ashes down the toilet.

Tess Whitehurst

July 10
Friday

4th ♉

Color of the day: Purple
Incense of the day: Alder

Lady Godiva's Ride

In 1040, it is said, Leofric, Lord of Coventry, laid onerous taxes upon his people. When his wife, Lady Godiva, begged him to be merciful, he challenged her: if she would ride naked through the town, he would rescind the taxes. This folktale may really be about the Celtic goddess Epona, and the purpose of her ride may have been to bestow the blessings of beauty and good fortune on the people.

What's going on in your world that needs correcting? With your eyes and mind open and focused, decide what needs to be done and what action you can best take. (You don't need to ride naked, though you may…) Invoke Epona and other goddesses for courage and strength, and take appropriate action to bring change into the world and restore its true beauty. Do practical and magical work for the environment, for people in need, or for animals.

Barbara Ardinger, PhD

July 11
Saturday

4th ♉

☽ v/c 5:52 pm
☽ → ♊ 8:16 pm

Color of the day: Indigo
Incense of the day: Sandalwood

Working with Bonfires

A bonfire is a large fire usually designed for celebration or to transmit a signal over a long distance. The word comes from "bone fire," a reference to the use of large fires to burn human bones, as in times of plague.

For Witches and Pagans today, bonfires are typically joyous occasions and often follow the Wheel of the Year, but you can use a bonfire for other events, too. Like all fires, the bonfire itself mimics ritual energy—from the quiet intentional lighting, to the rising energy of the flames, and then to the ebbing, grounding of the soft coals.

Begin your ritual magick with an ordered, ceremonial laying of the wood and a practiced fire-lighting. Then let your ritual work follow the fire's energy. Finish by sitting fireside, scrying into the flames or watching heat-shapes dance through the fading coals.

Susan Pesznecker

July 12
Sunday

4th ♊

Color of the day: Amber
Incense of the day: Hyacinth

Refreshing Lime Spell

By this date, for most people in the Northern Hemisphere, the summer heat has set in. Here is a spell to add a bit of refreshment and solar energy to your Sun-day. While many may think of oranges first when thinking of solar fruits, limes also resonate with solar energy and add a cool burst to many summer dishes and drinks. Take a lime and hold it up toward the sun. Say a blessing such as the following:

Blessed fruit of the sun,

Bring us the energy of the great solar one.

Green fruit of healing and regeneration,

Add to our drinks a cool refreshing sensation.

By the divine solar power within thee,

Blessed be!

Cut a lime into wedges and add one to your favorite summer drink. Visualize your energy being replenished and bolstered by the cool, refreshing solar-influenced citrus fruit.

Blake Octavian Blair

July 13
Monday

4th ♊
☽ v/c 11:31 pm

Color of the day: Gray
Incense of the day: Rosemary

Sunflower Seed Snack Balls

Sunflowers make me think of the fiery heat of the summer sun. These little snacks are not only a great way to embrace the element of fire, but are also a healthy pick-me-up during a hectic day. As you mix and roll the balls, think of the sunflowers eagerly following the sun as it crosses the sky. You will need:

- 1 cup old fashioned oats (not quick)
- ½ cup ground flax seed
- ½ cup nut butter
- ⅓ cup honey, preferably local
- 1 ½ teaspoons vanilla
- ½ cup mini chocolate chips
- ½ cup sunflower seeds

This is so easy—dump it all into a bowl and mix well with a spoon. Refrigerate for a half hour so it's firmer and easier to handle, then roll into one-inch balls of yumminess. Store in the fridge.

As you form the dough into balls, try to focus on the healing, nurturing warmth of the sun.

Laurel Reufner

July 14
Tuesday

4th ♊

☽ → ♋ 2:14 am

Color of the day: White
Incense of the day: Basil

A Thunderstorm Spell

A July thunderstorm is awesome. The thunder, lightning, and rain can be a dramatic spectacle, but thunderstorms also have a cleansing effect. They clear away dust, heat, and humidity.

Magically, we can use the power of a thunderstorm to cleanse our living space. For this spell, you'll need your magic broom. If you see a storm approaching, open your windows and doors, and see and feel any dark energy in your home breaking up until it has no power. See it being blown or drawn out of every window or door.

Now take your broom, and sweep vigorously out your front door and away from your home. Do the same at the back door. If possible, catch a few raindrops in your hand, and anoint your front and back thresholds. If safety is an issue, close your windows and doors. Then after the storm, open up your house again.

James Kambos

July 15
Wednesday

4th ♋

New Moon 9:24 pm

Color of the day: Yellow
Incense of the day: Honeysuckle

Wicked Tryst Spell

For this spell, assemble:

- One willing tantric lover
- One bottle of vodka
- One vanilla bean and seeds, halved and scraped
- Two sticks of cinnamon
- One tablespoon fresh ground ginger
- One fresh jalapeno, sliced
- Two single serving bags of horny goat weed tea, brewed in three fluid ounces boiling water
- Himalayan pink salt, for a tantric garnish
- Limes, for a juicy garnish

To spice up that summer fling, serve up a wicked tryst to celebrate the season of fun in the Sol. Pour out two shots of vodka, and toss each of them onto your bed as an offering to Venus, the goddess of love, and her eternal lover, Mars.

Brew the tea in three fluid ounces of boiling water, and set aside for twenty minutes. Into the bottle, place the brewed tea, vanilla bean, cinnamon sticks, ground ginger, and sliced jalapeno. Shake the bottle vigorously while you envision, with creative diversity, the pornographic results that this tincture promises.

Place the vodka bottle in the freezer and chill for two hours. Garnish the serving glasses with freshly crushed Himalayan pink salt to invoke the highest climbs of tantric eroticism. Serve this spiced liquor cold, with a twist of lime. Temper the mood a bit by mixing with pink grapefruit sparkling citrus water or ginger ale.

Estha McNevin

NOTES:

July 16
Thursday

NOTES:

1st ♋

☽ v/c 7:24 am

☽ → ♌ 10:15 am

Color of the day: Purple
Incense of the day: Balsam

The Womanly Power of Red

There is no denying the power of red. It is the color of fire, power, and passion. It can add energy to your spells and cure dead zones in your home. Crystals hung at the windows with red ribbons or thread ward off bad spirits and invite good into your life.

Every month at around the time of the new moon (yesterday), groups of women across the country gather together under the umbrella of the Red Tent Temple Movement. No children (except for the smallest of babies) are allowed in circle, and no men. Here, women find comfort and companionship, sisterhood and sanctuary. Participants share lively conversation, refreshments, and occasionally crafts, and the day ends with chanting and song and dance to honor the goddess in all women. With dozens of Red Tent Temple chapters across the country, there is sure to be one near you. Or you may wish to start a chapter on your own.

Emyme

July 17
Friday

1st ♍

Color of the day: Rose
Incense of the day: Orchid

Crown Yourself with Glory

This spell aids success at work, at home, and in other parts of life. You will need:

- A 6 × 6-inch piece of golden fabric
- A golden charm of a crown
- A nugget of amber resin (about pea size)
- A cat's-eye stone (pea size or larger)
- High John the Conqueror root (about half an inch of whole root or a pinch of ground)
- A pinch of deer's tongue leaves
- A pinch of five finger grass
- A red ribbon

First lay out the fabric with the charm in the center. Add the amber resin, saying:

May I have the soul of a tiger in pursuing my goals.

Add the cat's-eye stone, saying:

May everyone look on me with the eyes of a friend.

Add the High John the Conqueror root, saying:

May I command power.

Add the deer's tongue leaves, saying:

May I speak convincingly.

Add the five finger grass, saying:

May I succeed in all my endeavors.

Hold the bundle closed, saying:

So I claim my power;
everything I do is crowned in glory.

Remove the crown to carry with you. Tie the cloth around the remaining items with a red ribbon, and keep it in a safe place.

Elizabeth Barrette

NOTES:

July 18
Saturday

1st ♌

☽ v/c 5:41 pm

☽ → ♍ 8:47 pm

Color of the day: Blue
Incense of the day: Rue

Uncrossing Your Path

An uncrossing bath is used to wash away whatever personal issues may be blocking your path to personal growth.

Draw a warm tub of water, and light your bath with candles. Burn incense to smudge away any personal debris that you carry with you. You want an environment that will enable you to meditate on finding what is stopping you from achieving your goals, ways to remove or resolve the issue, and how to recover your balance and move forward with your life.

Herbs and/or oils to use in your bath can be sage to cleanse and remove the blockage, rose for healing, and peppermint to move forward with your life. But any combination of herbs to clean, heal, and motivate can be used, depending on your preferences and/or allergies.

Boudica

July 19
Sunday

1st ♍

Color of the day: Orange
Incense of the day: Frankincense

Friendship Talisman

Gather a piece of moonstone, rose quartz, or jade (or all three) and a violet or ivy leaf. Wrap these in a small piece of green fabric, and, as you assemble the bundle, think of a friend you wish to form a closer bond with, either emotionally or because there is a geographic distance between you. Alternately, you may use this spell to seek more friends or deepen existing friendships. Concentrate on your desire as you pull the sides of the fabric together and tie three knots with a pink ribbon. Sprinkle the bundle with three drops of sandalwood, vanilla, or patchouli oil, and bury the bundle in a safe location, such as your garden or with a potted plant.

Ember Grant

July 20
Monday

1st ♍

Color of the day: White
Incense of the day: Hyssop

Money Conjure Bag

When you need money, a fast, effective, and inexpensive charm bag can be made by placing one bay leaf, one teaspoon allspice, and one coin (any currency) from the year you were born into a green or gold cloth bag and tying it shut with green or gold cord, whichever you feel most symbolizes money. Hold the bag over a green candle (carefully), anoint it with saltwater, and hold it in the smoke of allspice incense, saying the following to bind the charge:

> *Lucky coin and gifts from earth,*
>
> *Increase flow of money to me.*
>
> *Building up my net worth,*
>
> *Bringing me prosperity.*

Carry the bag with you and sleep with it under your pillow, if possible.

Michael Furie

July 21
Tuesday

1st ♍

☽ v/c 6:07 am
☽ → ♎ 9:23 am

Color of the day: Maroon
Incense of the day: Ylang-ylang

Raising Energy

The sun will enter Leo soon. We're moving from water to fire. Although heat and humidity often lead to lassitude, you can use a combination of watery and fiery powers to raise energy for work you want to do, either mundane or magical.

The workhorse of the nineteenth and early twentieth centuries was the steam engine. Steam engines were huge. They powered locomotives, riverboats, and factories. They made it possible to accomplish work that had previously required endless hard labor. Set your goal and state your intention to get the task you choose done. Write your goal in gold ink on a sheet of paper, and lay it on your altar. Next, fill yourself with fuel, both healthy food and the supplies you need. Now get to work. Visualize yourself as The Little Engine That Could:

> *I think I can.*
> *I think I can.*
> *I know I can!*

Barbara Ardinger, PhD

July 22
Wednesday

1st ♎

☉ → ♌ 11:30 pm

Color of the day: White
Incense of the day: Lilac

Simple home Bibliomancy

Gather a number of books, magazines, and pamphlets to use for this divination. This bibliomancy, or divination by way of books, may accompany a spell you are crafting to provide additional insight into the working at hand.

Write a series of questions on a large piece of paper, with room to write a "response" below each. In a private space, ask the universe to deliver you the insight you need for each issue or question.

With the stack of literature before you, close your eyes and repeat the first question in your head. At random, grab the piece of literature that you feel drawn toward. With your eyes still closed, turn to a random page and point your finger where you feel guided. When you're ready, open your eyes and see the phrase or words you are pointing at. Write this down as the "answer," and continue the process with each question. Afterward, use your creative mind to help interpret the symbolic messages.

Raven Digitalis

 July 23
Thursday

1st ♎

☽ v/c 2:12 pm
☽ → ♏ 10:07 pm

Color of the day: Crimson
Incense of the day: Mulberry

Neptunalia

Neptunalia is an ancient Roman festival lasting for two days and honoring Neptune, god of the waters. The holiday was celebrated at the height of the arid summer, when water was both scarce and precious. Neptunalia was a grand community event; people built temporary tents and shelters to protect them from the sun and engaged in games, races, and feasting.

You can create a Neptunalia for your friends! Share food, play games outdoors (badminton, croquet, bocce ball, horseshoes), and provide at least one shelter tent. A fountain, a water basin, or even a wading pool would be an appropriate focal element. At the celebration's peak, invite everyone into the tent to participate in a water-sharing ceremony, passing a consecrated pitcher of water and inviting everyone to fill their own cups. Drink to Neptune, proclaiming:

May we never thirst!

Susan Pesznecker

 July 24
Friday

1st ♏

2nd Quarter 12:04 am

Color of the day: Coral
Incense of the day: Yarrow

Spell of Balance

What are you growing in your inner garden? What are you nurturing? What no longer deserves or requires your energy and must be released? Now is the time to bring all into balance. For this spell, you'll need some small stones and some gold and black paint. Cast your circle, and for each thing you need to continue to nurture, paint a symbol or word on one of the stones in gold (or other "action" color). For each thing you do for yourself in order to rest or heal, paint a symbol or word on a stone in black (or other color of stillness or "non-action"). When you're finished, look at the two piles of stones, pick them up, and hold them in your hands. Do they balance? If not, why not? Do you need more self-care or more actions in your life? Which of these actions could be discarded, delegated, or set aside for another time? When all have been assessed, line the stones up on your altar in an alternating pattern to remind you of the balance that keeps your life healthy and nurturing to you. Blessed be.

Thuri Calafia

 July 25
Saturday

2nd ♏

Color of the day: Black
Incense of the day: Pine

Mermaid House Blessing

Mermaids help with emotional healing, sensuality, and wealth. They can also help move the energy around in our homes in a beautifully fluid way. For this purpose, obtain a statue of a mermaid or mermaids. Display it in a central location or near the entrance. Place a glass bowl of water near it, along with three white candles. Anoint the candles with ylang-ylang oil and light. Place one teaspoon sea salt in the water, and stir in a clockwise direction. Place one hand on your heart and one on your belly. Breathe and relax as you envision the deep blue sea moving through every room and area of your home, swirling, bubbling, and washing away the old. Then say:

> Mermaids, I call on you and invite you in. Thank you for cleansing this home and for blessing us with your beautiful, sensual presence. You are welcome here. Thank you.

Tess Whitehurst

July 26
Sunday

2nd ♏

☽ v/c 5:14 am

☽ → ♐ 8:24 am

Color of the day: Gold
Incense of the day: Heliotrope

There and Back Again

Summertime sees scores of people hitting the roads, rails, and skies for vacation, work, conventions, and festivals. Perform this spell for safe travel, whether you're going on a far-flung trip or your daily commute.

Log in to your favorite online service to create a map of your route, being sure to include all the stops you plan to make. Using a black marker (black for protection), trace your route, visualizing yourself arriving at each destination safely. Next, with broad outward strokes, color the route with a blue highlighter, giving your path a protective aura in case of detours or change of plans. Lastly, write this mantra out along your route:

From here to there and back,

Safe and sound and right on track.

Keep the map with you when you travel. Safe journeys!

Natalie Zaman

 July 27
Monday

2nd ♐

Color of the day: Silver
Incense of the day: Narcissus

Protective Onion Braid

Onions ripen in late summer to autumn, depending on the variety and location. This vegetable is associated with protection and purification. Onions represent eternal life according to Egyptian tradition.

You can protect your home by making an onion braid. You need at least six onions complete with their tops. (If you don't grow your own, sometimes you can find whole onions with tops at a farmers' market or natural food store.) Double up a piece of twine and knot a loop in the middle for hanging. Use this to support the onions as you braid them together, adding one onion at a time. Concentrate on protection as you work.

When the braid is done, you can attach protective charms to the twine, such as the Eye of Horus or scarab beetle from Egypt, cornicello from Italy, ahimsa hand from Jainism, or the Wiccan pentacle.

Elizabeth Barrette

July 28
Tuesday

2nd ♐

☽ v/c 9:36 am

☽ → ♑ 2:47 pm

Color of the day: Black
Incense of the day: Ginger

hand Wash for Abundance

Make an infusion by steeping fresh basil leaves in boiling water. Cool and strain (or brew using a cheesecloth bundle or tea bag), and use this water to wash your hands. Add it to liquid soap in a pump bottle, or simply sprinkle it onto your hands as you wash them. Visualize money flowing easily to you, bills being paid with ease, and abundance for everything else you need. Repeat this simple chant to seal the spell:

Money, money, come to me,

With harm to none, so mote it be!

Ember Grant

July 29
Wednesday

2nd ♑

Color of the day: Brown
Incense of the day: Marjoram

Color Me Creative

Sometimes the creativity well runs dry, or you just need some time away from a project while your mind works through a problem. Many of us enjoy folding laundry or maybe washing dishes at such moments, but there are certainly other, more enjoyable ways to take a break. One of my favorites is to color. It occupies both your hands and the main part of your focus while whatever it is you need to puzzle over sits there on the back burner, simmering away.

When you feel the need, light a purple candle, pull out a special coloring book or pages printed from the Internet, and grab your crayon box. Spend at least an hour just coloring and relaxing. Enjoy choosing the colors you use, and see how they interact with each other on the page. And let your mind wander.

Laurel Reufner

July 30
Thursday

2nd ♑

☽ v/c 2:50 pm

☽ → ♒ 5:40 pm

Color of the day: Turquoise
Incense of the day: Jasmine

Reciprocity for Prosperity

Thursday's Jupiterian influences make it a great day for working on the ever-practical magick of prosperity. Procure a stone aligned with prosperity, such as citrine or green jade, along with three dollar bills. Rub each dollar bill onto the stone while reciting the following incantation:

Dollar bills, three by three,

Sent into the world,

You bring prosperity back to me.

By principle of reciprocity,

So mote it be!

Now, keep the stone in your pocket, wallet, purse, or business's cash drawer. Take the dollar bills and spend them during the course of today. Know with confidence—through the magickal principle of reciprocity—that by sharing prosperity, you too shall be prosperous.

Blake Octavian Blair

July 31
Friday

2nd ♒

Full Moon 6:43 am

Color of the day: White
Incense of the day: Mint

Day of Uncommon Instruments

Uncommon instruments—from ancient times, or from countries other than our own, or those that we invent—include:

- the didgeridoo—a long wooden trumpet
- the daxophone—a wooden blade attached to a wooden block with contact microphones
- the bubble organ—made from balloons, water, old furniture, and rain gutters
- the aquaggaswack—tuned pot lids welded onto plumbing pipes

Research "uncommon instruments" on the Internet for more examples, and visit www.vegetableorchestra.org for a truly inventive treat.

After all this inspiration, fashion your own uncommon instrument. Children are instinctively creative, so include them in this exercise.

Then say:

Light the spark,

Greet the muse,

Open the channel,

Ideas flow through.

Emyme

Notes:

August

The eighth calendar month is full of the last hurrahs of summer (or winter, if you're in the Southern Hemisphere). Originally the sixth month of the Roman calendar, August was known as Sextilis until the Senate changed it to Augustus sometime around 8 BC. This was in honor of Augustus Caesar. August was full of holidays. The month started with a public festival honoring Spes, the goddess of hope, and ended with the Charisteria, a feast in which to give thanks. Most of the deities honored in August were fertility and harvest gods. The Anglo-Saxons referred to August as Weod Monath (Weed Month) or Arn-monath (Barn Month). In the Northern Hemisphere, August marks the start of the harvest season festivals, with the celebration of Lughnassad, or Lammas, on the 1st. August starts out in the constellation of Leo, a fixed fire sign, and moves into Virgo, a mutable earth sign, around the 20th. The birthstone of the month is peridot. Interesting fun fact: No other month starts on the same day of the week as August unless it's a leap year, in which case August and February start on the same day.

Laurel Reufner

August 1

Saturday

3rd ♒

☽ v/c 6:02 pm

☽ → ♓ 6:36 pm

Color of the day: Brown

Incense of the day: Ivy

Lammas

Celebrating the Fruits of Our Labor

First harvest usually celebrates the ripening and picking of berries and grains. To celebrate, make some fresh berry jam and bread. Or if you are like me, you know all the right stores to pick up a fresh, hot loaf of bread and some freshly made jams.

For this solitary ritual, the meal is some slices of the fresh bread spread with the jam. At this time of harvesting foods, many of us are harvesting success in our jobs, projects, or work, and have much to celebrate in the way of gathering the fruits of our labors. The bread and jam will represent all those good things that have come to us this year, be it the ability to pay our bills or greater success with our projects.

I am not a big fan of leaving human food for wild animals. So sit in a park, open your lunch box, pull out the jam-spread bread, and enjoy the meal in the comfort of nature while contemplating your joys.

Salute Mother Nature, your favorite god or goddess, or the universe for all the little things that have made your life easier.

Boudica

NOTES:

August 2
Sunday

3rd ♓

Color of the day: Orange
Incense of the day: Eucalyptus

Manifest a helping hand

Pull the Ace of Wands from your tarot deck. Place it on the center of your main altar. Next to it place a full-size wax figure of a right hand, to your right. Throughout the working, maintain direct and steady eye contact with the Ace of Wands; think of your survival, but look only at the ace. When you are ready, flood the room with candlelight, keeping your eyes locked on the tarot card. Then settle down before your altar to begin the working.

In a shocking, violent, and sudden motion, reach for and grasp the wax hand without taking your eyes off the card. Make this action filled with fear and the unawareness of what you are grappling for, as if you were falling from a great height and grasping your only chance at survival, when another human reaches out a hand to save your life. Envision this scenario strongly as you chant the following invocation ten times:

Palm to palm and breath to breath,
help me before I've nothing left. By the
hand of glory and the fist of the forge,
grant me strength through support
paid forward.

When your work is done, return the card to your deck and leave the wax hand to rest on your altar or in a special place in your home to draw more support into your life.

Estha McNevin

NOTES:

August 3

Monday

3rd ♓

☽ v/c 4:35 pm

☽ → ♈ 7:24 pm

Color of the day: Silver
Incense of the day: Rosemary

A Sachet Against Drama

Life's dramas can be overwhelming, especially when you desire peacefulness in your interactions. While it may be said that every experience happens for a reason, in order to spiritually teach life lessons, some of life's lessons can be learned without the heavy amounts of gossip or slander that may accompany them. Tonight's waning moon assists in this spell.

Fill an all-natural, biodegradable sachet bag or small paper bag with the herbs slippery elm, rue, and yarrow. Add one piece of hematite to the bag. In a sacred space, burn a yellow candle and a black candle to symbolize the end of gossip and drama. Staring at the bag, begin to recite every dramatic, slanderous, gossipy phrase that you've heard recently—anything and everything that comes to mind! Allow your mind and mouth to race a thousand miles a minute; your goal is to direct this socially confusing energy into the sachet so that it can be destroyed.

When you feel your work is done, punch your fist into the bag and then spit on the bag. Say:

*Gone! Drama banished! Gossip halted!
Slander stopped! It is done!*

Bury the bag somewhere on your property to guard against future incidents.

Raven Digitalis

NOTES:

August 4
Tuesday

3rd ♈

Color of the day: White
Incense of the day: Cinnamon

Spell of Sacrifice

At this time of sacred harvest, while still mindful of all that Lugh gave up to save his people, we are called upon to think about what we're willing to give up for the betterment of our own lives and those of our loved ones. Take some time to go through your closets, pantry, garage, even your altar, and ask yourself which of these items you've used in the past year, or even the past season. Do you really need so much stuff? Pile all of these beloved unused treasures near a box. Then, one by one, take a moment with each thing, cleansing it of any negative energies it may still have, then energizing it with good wishes and memories, blessing whoever its next owner will be with all the abundance and positivity those memories hold. Finally, take the box to a favorite charity, and be blessed.

Thuri Calafia

August 5
Wednesday

3rd ♈

☽ v/c 7:29 pm
☽ → ♉ 9:29 pm

Color of the day: Yellow
Incense of the day: Honeysuckle

August Prosperity Spell

Wheat, which is one of the grains being harvested this month, is associated with the Goddess and wealth. Draw prosperity to you by casting this spell. Have on hand enough wheat bran to form a circle around you. If possible, perform this spell outdoors. Sit and center yourself. Feel as if you're rooted to the earth. Think of at least three things you're thankful for and say them aloud. Now stand and begin to sprinkle the wheat bran around you so that you're completely surrounded by it. Sit once again and say this prayer:

Lord and Lady, I thank you for what I have.

I ask you to keep me surrounded with prosperity.

May abundance continue to flow into my life.

Inhale deeply and release. Step out of the circle, and leave the wheat as a thank you to Mother Earth. The spell is done.

James Kambos

August 6
Thursday

3rd ♉

4th Quarter 10:03 pm

Color of the day: Crimson

Incense of the day: Clove

Becoming Stronger

Thursday is ruled by Thor, the hammer-wielding Norse god of strength and protection who corresponds (more or less) to Jupiter, king of the Roman gods. In Greek mythology, the Titan who rules Thursday is Eurymedon ("wide-ruling"); the Titaness is Themis ("order").

In what part of your life do you need to be stronger? Set images of Thor, Jupiter, and the Titans on your altar. If you have a Thor's hammer amulet, hold it in your stronger hand. (You can hold a real hammer, but be very careful.) Obeying the Wiccan Rede ("harm none") and knowing that we must not do magic that coerces other people to bow before us, invoke Thor and Jupiter and ask them to stand beside you (or "have your back") where you require strength. Invoke Themis and ask her to remind you that order is often superior to strength. Feel strength and order flowing into your mind and arms.

Barbara Ardinger, PhD

August 7
Friday

4th ♉

Color of the day: Purple

Incense of the day: Rose

Dragon's Eye Protection Spell

If you feel the need for magical protection, you can use this simple and effective candle spell. On the upper half of a red candle, carve a symbol known as the "dragon's eye," which is a downward-pointing triangle with a "Y" shape in the middle, making a pyramid. This is said to be a symbol of making choices and giving direction. Beneath this symbol on the lower half of the candle, carve an upward-pointing pentagram; thus you are directing protection. Anoint the candle with dragon's blood oil and charge it with protective energy. As you light the candle, visualize its energy surrounding you with an impenetrable shield of protection, and say the following to seal the spell:

Dragon's eye and pentagram, cast all evil away.

Powers of protection, now encircle me,

Guard me night and guard me day,

Safe and secure, I shall be.

Michael Furie

August 8

Saturday

4th ♉

☽ v/c 12:46 am

☽ → ♊ 1:40 am

Color of the day: Black

Incense of the day: Patchouli

Spell to Banish Debt

Most everyone has some kind of debt to overcome, whether it's student loans, credit cards, or just regular bills. Collect statements of debts owed, and mark an "X" on them with black ink. Then cut them into very small pieces, letting the pieces fall in a pile. Visualize the debt being cut until nothing remains—you are free of the financial burden.

Place the paper pieces in the bottom of a heatproof container, and place a black votive candle on top of them. Light the candle and allow it to burn completely and cool. The wax will have covered the paper and bound it. Remove wax and paper, and bury them where they won't be disturbed. Forget about them. Pay the bills, but bury the worry.

Ember Grant

 August 9

Sunday

4th ♊

Color of the day: Yellow

Incense of the day: Juniper

Living Fire

The fire element is the liveliest of the four cardinal elements and is associated with passion and intensity. While the planet Earth is our home, it was born of fire: the fires of volcanism and those of the universe, with stellar explosions providing atomic elements to make life possible. The fire element is one of vigor, enthusiasm, and creation.

Spend a day—or longer—focusing deeply on your connection to the fire element. Dress in colors of red, orange, and gold, and wear silks or laboratory-spun fibers if you can. Carry bloodstone, amber, carnelian, or jasper—stones powerfully associated with fire, energy, and courage. Spend an evening meditating around a campfire or hearth fire and cooking your meal over the flames. Practice fire-scrying: gaze into the flames, ask meaningful questions, and open your mind to answers. Give thanks for the blessings of fire!

Susan Pesznecker

August 10
Monday

4th ♊

☽ v/c 7:45 am

☽ → ♋ 8:08 am

Color of the day: Lavender

Incense of the day: Lily

Cool Down Spell

Heat is good. It heals, purifies, and gives comfort. Here at the height of summer, heat is expected—but too much of anything can be dangerous and unhealthy. Balance physical and mental heat (it's so easy to get "hot and bothered" at this time of the year!) with this spell. Performing it now, when the moon is waning, will also help to "shrink" the heat. You will need a spray bottle, ice, water, and some mint leaves.

Fill the bottle with the ice, water, and mint. Swirl it in a counterclockwise motion for banishing, and speak this mantra:

Coolness is green,

Fresh, and clean.

Away worry, anger, and heat.

Between hot and cool, summer is sweet!

Spray the water on yourself, and feel its coolness washing over you. Keep the spray bottle in the refrigerator and spritz yourself (and plants and animals) whenever you need to.

Natalie Zaman

August 11
Tuesday

4th ♋

Color of the day: Black

Incense of the day: Bayberry

Saint Clare Day

Whether or not you're inspired by Catholic iconography, if you take a moment to tune in to the energy of the spiritual helper known as Saint Clare of Assisi—a dear friend and colleague of Saint Francis—you'll find that she possesses very clean, clear, powerful, and loving vibrations. She is the unofficial saint of clairvoyance, and some Vodou traditions associate her with mermaids and the moon. Clare wrote: "Place your mind before the mirror of eternity! Place your soul in the brilliance of glory! And transform your entire being into the image of the Godhead Itself through contemplation."

Today, honor Saint Clare and hone your intuitive gifts by calling on her, lighting a white candle, and contemplating the Infinite while gazing softly into a mirror. Say:

Saint Clare, I call on you! Thank you for bringing out my psychic gifts and aligning my mind with All That Is. Thank you.

Tess Whitehurst

August 12
Wednesday

4th ♋

☽ v/c 1:44 pm

☽ → ♌ 4:52 pm

Color of the day: White
Incense of the day: Lavender

The Magick of Crayons

Basic artistic representation is an ancient pastime—think of the cave drawings of Lascaux. Simple toys are the best, those that call out the creativity in all ages. Crayons marry these two truths in a most colorful and powerful way. Consider the myriad ways crayons can be and are used in our modern world. A study has shown the scent of crayons to be one of the most recognizable in the world. How can such an object not be infused with magic? Coloring books and crayons are enjoyed by children of all ages and are used as therapy for many ailments.

Whether you grew up with many crayons or few, honor your magickal inner child today and purchase a box of these marvelous waxy sticks. Treat yourself to drawing paper or a coloring book. Lose yourself in the rainbow. Say:

I will play today,
And let my mind relax
Back to childhood.

Iris, goddess of rainbows,
Inspire me as you did
Those inventors of crayons.

Emyme

NOTES:

August 13

Thursday

4th ♌

Color of the day: Green
Incense of the day: Carnation

Finding Hope

Life's happenings can sometimes seem depressingly overwhelming. Then we need to take a step back and find reasons to keep going—to have hope.

Use some jasmine oil (fragrance oil works) to dress deep blue and silver candles. With the candles set before you, pull out a notebook and a pen that you like. On the left-hand side of a page, list as many things about your life currently that have you feeling like you are drowning. Now on the right-hand side, list a positive to match as many of those negatives as you can. You may not get very far at first, but this is the kind of ritual you can come back to as often as necessary. When you start to grasp for hope, review that list of positives and continue on.

Laurel Reufner

 August 14

Friday

4th ♌
New Moon 10:53 am

Color of the day: Pink
Incense of the day: Violet

New Moon

The new moon—or dark moon, as some call it—is a time of waning energy. Work in sync with the new moon by planning quiet, low-energy activities during those two or three days each month. Stay close to home, keep the house cool and dark, plan simple meals, and use the time to evaluate your various projects and begin planning new ones. Work magicks that focus on manifestation, growth, and new beginnings, for the period beginning with the new moon and extending toward the full moon is ideal for these practices. Don't forget to sleep! Most people find they sleep like rocks when the moon is dark and the energies are low. Living in sync with the lunar cycles is a great way to live your life in rhythm with the universe around you. May the dark moon's gifts be yours!

Susan Pesznecker

August 15

Saturday

1st ♌

☽ v/c 12:36 am

☽ → ♍ 3:46 am

Color of the day: Blue
Incense of the day: Sage

Enjoy Relaxation Day

Today is Relaxation Day. This holiday gives people a chance to unwind and pamper themselves (or each other). It is widely celebrated by spas, massage therapists, yoga centers, and other branches of the personal service sector. However, people often observe Relaxation Day at home with a bubble bath, a picnic, or a nap in a hammock.

If you don't already have a meditation corner at home, today is a great time to make one. It can be as simple as a cushion or yoga mat to sit on, a mandala poster, some soothing incense, and/or an album of trance music. Sit down and concentrate on tensing and then relaxing your body, a little at a time, starting with your feet. Relax your mind by meditating on peace and calm.

Remember that even though there is a holiday for relaxation, this is really something you should do regularly.

Elizabeth Barrette

 August 16

Sunday

1st ♍

Color of the day: Gold
Incense of the day: Almond

Home Blessing and Reconsecration

On this date in 1891 was the inauguration and blessing of the Basilica of San Sebastian in Manila, Philippines, the only all-steel church in Asia. Take this anniversary as a cue to remember that our homes are also sacred sanctuaries worthy of blessing. Even if you have lived in your home for many years and have already blessed it, a home can never have too many blessings, so enjoy performing a reconsecration! Gather a representation of each element, such as blessed sea-salt water for earth and water, smudge or incense for air and fire, and a bell or rattle for spirit. Make a round through your home with each element, wafting, sprinkling, and ringing/rattling as appropriate. Repeat a simple blessing during the process such as:

I bless this home as sacred space.

May divine love dwell within this place.

Blake Octavian Blair

August 17
Monday

1st ♍︎

☽ v/c 1:16 pm

☽ → ♎︎ 4:23 pm

Color of the day: Ivory
Incense of the day: Hyssop

Healing Old Wounds

We may be carrying around some extra emotional baggage that is the result of being hurt by a family member, a close friend, or someone we trusted who betrayed our trust. The focus is not on those things we caused, but those things that were clearly caused by others.

These old wounds need to heal. Some wounds may never heal completely. Many people choose to seek professional help with these issues, and it is always recommended not to go this road alone.

It is not always our fault that these things happened, and forgiveness is not always the answer. In many cases, we can never forgive, and it should not be expected of us.

But we can forgive ourselves. In the end, we need to forgive ourselves. We need to put the past in the past and move forward with our lives. We cannot live in our mistakes. We are survivors, not victims.

Boudica

August 18
Tuesday

1st ♎︎

Color of the day: Scarlet
Incense of the day: Geranium

Auspicious Golden Box

Find a golden cardboard box (large enough to fit business cards), or paint a wooden box metallic gold. Hold it in both hands and say:

I am very well connected. I have friends in high places. Everyone I know is helpful, and I am always meeting helpful people. Auspicious connections are everywhere for me, now and always.

Visualize the box filled with golden light. Place it in the "helpful people" feng shui area of your home (when you are facing your home from the entrance, the right corner closest to the front or entrance of the home). Whenever you receive a business card of someone with whom you would like to share a mutually beneficial connection, place it in the box. Similarly, if you interview for a job somewhere or would like to have positive dealings with a certain business, procure one of their cards and place it in the box.

Tess Whitehurst

August 19
Wednesday

1st ♎

☽ v/c 10:56 pm

Color of the day: Brown
Incense of the day: Bay laurel

Fruit Tree Charms

Throughout the harvest season, many Pagans practice a technique of offering energy, prayers, fertilizer, or love to a fruit tree before it is harvested. However, not all fruit in our grocery stores is treated with the same honor. This spell is designed to give love and gratitude to any fruit tree you see.

From a craft supply or bead store, procure some fruit-shaped glass beads; some white lace agate beads for peace, grace, and gratitude; and some blue labradorite beads for hope, spiritual vision, and healing. Finally, select a variety of brass bells, each different in pitch and size.

Make the fruit charms using cold-weather fishing line. First, create a large loop to slip-knot around a tree branch. Then thread the beads in patterns that you like. End each charm with a bell, and take a moment to imbue each with loving gratitude.

Throughout the day, give the charms as offerings to any fruit trees that you know and love or to any auspicious fruit trees that you stumble upon. In the moment that you hang the charm, thank the tree for holding all of the fruitful wisdom of Mother Earth.

Estha McNevin

Notes:

August 20

Thursday

1st ♎

☽ → ♏ 5:24 am

Color of the day: Turquoise
Incense of the day: Balsam

Study Candle Spell

For many folks, summer's end heralds school's beginning, and even those of us not embarking on college courses usually have studies and courses we wish to pursue. For this spell, you'll need a pillar candle in the color you most associate with the mind (yellow is most common). Carve the candle with symbols and words that mean alertness and study to you, as well as symbols of success and clarity. Anoint the candle with oils of rosemary and walnut (for mental powers) while saying these words:

All I need to know is coming through to me clearly, easily, and completely. This information stays in my brain and can be accessed by me at any time. So mote it be.

Seal the candle with some spell sealing oil and light it whenever you study.

Thuri Calafia

 August 21

Friday

1st ♏

Color of the day: White
Incense of the day: Alder

A Working to Increase Objectivity

It's easy to get overwhelmed in life. It's difficult not to absorb other people's opinions or perceptions as one's own. For that reason, objectivity—rather than subjectivity—is an ideal approach to take in life. This can allow a person to see more sides of a situation and feel less emotionally invested in any given challenge.

To help encourage objectivity, fill a small sachet bag with the herbs rue, rosemary, peppermint, yarrow, and salt. For extra oomph, add some black tourmaline. In a sacred space, hold this bag to your mouth and whisper to it:

Bag of life, bag of light, guard my perception through day and through night. My mind is aware while my thoughts arise; I discern objectivity through my eyes.

Repeat this four times.

Finally, brush the bag through the elements: dirt, flame, incense smoke, and water. Carry it on your person whenever you need objectivity in life.

Raven Digitalis

♈ August 22

Saturday

1st ♏

☽ v/c 3:31 pm

2nd Quarter 3:31 pm

☽ → ♐ 4:41 pm

Color of the day: Gray

Incense of the day: Rue

A harvest Queen Spell

During colonial times, farmers would frequently fashion a human figure out of grain known as the "Harvest Queen," to show their thanks for a bountiful harvest. With this spell, you'll be able to do the same and take part in an age-old custom.

To make your Harvest Queen, you'll need long stems of grasses, grain, perhaps some corn husks, and garden twine. Make your figure anyway you wish. Use the garden twine to tie the plant materials together. The corn husks may be used to fashion a skirt or apron around the bottom of the figure. Use your imagination. As you make the figure, keep in mind how grateful you are for your garden's bounty.

When done, as a gesture of thanks, sprinkle the figure with water. Display the figure in the garden for a few days. Let it dry; in the spring, turn it into the soil.

James Kambos

 ♈ August 23

Sunday

2nd ♐

☉ → ♍ 6:37 am

Color of the day: Amber

Incense of the day: Marigold

Like a Virgo

Today the sun enters the sign of Virgo. Known for their attention to detail and well-thought-out decisions, Virgos are born grounded. Virgo might not be your sun sign, but you can channel her energy by putting on a piece of the Goddess.

Select at least one article of clothing in Virgo colors: green and brown are earthy, while deep blue is a nod to sapphire, Virgo's birthstone. Stand tall in front of a mirror as you dress or put on your Virgo accessory. Watch and listen to yourself as you say this spell:

Like a Virgo,

My feet are on the ground, my eyes are sharp.

My mind is meticulous, and loyal my heart.

Look in a mirror throughout the day to renew your connection to Virgo energy, sharpen your focus, and maintain balance.

Natalie Zaman

August 24
Monday

2nd ♐

☽ v/c 6:04 pm

Color of the day: White
Incense of the day: Clary sage

Magical Massage

A simple way to relax your muscles is to give yourself an energy massage. To do this, lie down on a bed on your stomach and focus on your breathing. Visualize energy coming up from the earth and entering your body through your feet when you inhale. Visualize white light moving from your feet, traveling up through your legs and back and to the top of your head during your inhale. On the exhale, send the energy back down through your body. As you are breathing and moving the energy through you, mentally use the energy to massage your muscles. Will that the energy relaxes your muscles as it travels. With a little practice, you should be able to feel the energy massage working. To end the exercise, do one final exhale, sending all the energy out of the soles of your feet and visualize it sinking back into the earth.

Michael Furie

 August 25
Tuesday

2nd ♐

☽ → ♑ 12:22 am

Color of the day: Gray
Incense of the day: Cedar

Mojo for Dream Recall

Tuesday's energies resonate well with red jasper. This wonderful earthy stone offers the perfect amount of grounding to provide protection without "holding you down." This is one of the reasons that this stone is wonderful for dream recall.

Make a simple mojo bag for good sleep and dream recall by placing a piece of red jasper and a couple spoons of lavender buds on a scrap of fabric. Then draw the corners together and tie with a ribbon. Place it under your pillow before going to sleep. Be sure to keep a notepad or journal next to your bed to record your dreams upon waking.

Blake Octavian Blair

August 26
Wednesday

2nd ♑

Color of the day: Topaz
Incense of the day: Lilac

Sing a Song

Today is sacred to the Finnish sky and air goddess Ilmatar, mother of Väinämöinen, who is said in the Kalevala to be the god of songs and poetry. People of all faiths love their songs and chants. As we sing, we send our energy through the air and into the ears of other people. It's good to send music into the atmosphere.

Make a list of your favorite songs and chants. Start with songs from your childhood—nursery rhymes, play songs, hymns, even Christmas carols. Add the songs you learned in school, songs you sang as you played your air guitar, songs you sang along with at concerts. Add your favorite chants. Where do these songs and chants take you? On days when you're feeling down, sing a song. Sing it loud and strong and sing it into your heart and out into the world. Let musical energy enliven the world.

Barbara Ardinger, PhD

August 27
Thursday

2nd ♑

☽ v/c 3:20 am

☽ → ♒ 4:03 am

Color of the day: Purple
Incense of the day: Myrrh

Giving Spell

There is a widely held belief in the Craft that what you do comes back to you. Generosity is something we can never have too much of in the world. Today, be generous. Use this spell to increase the spirit of generosity within you, that it may spread outward and inspire others. Donate something today, such as money or goods to charity, or donate your time as a volunteer. The good you do will come back to you.

Light a purple or white candle and recite the following:

Giving for the good of all,

Start with me, hear my call.

Giving will enrich our lives,

Giving strengthens all our ties.

Ember Grant

August 28

Friday

2nd ♒

Color of the day: Rose
Incense of the day: Mint

In the Moment

This is an all-day meditation, or perhaps ritual, to promote mindfulness. It's a way to help you be more present in the moment.

You will need a white pillar candle dedicated to Kwan Yin. If possible, dress the candle with ylang-ylang or mimosa oil. When you arise in the morning, light the candle and sit quietly before it for a few minutes before going about the rest of your day. Your goal for the day is to stay present in what is happening within and around you as you go about your activities. If your mind starts to wander to your to-do lists, relationship worries, or plans for the weekend (you get the idea here), take a moment to ground and bring yourself back to the present. At the end of the day, spend a few more minutes in front of the candle, being thankful for all you noticed.

Laurel Reufner

 ## August 29

Saturday

2nd ♒

☽ v/c 3:03 am
☽ → ♓ 4:51 am
Full Moon 2:35 pm

Color of the day: Black
Incense of the day: Ivy

Water Energy Alignment

Pisces is the most watery of signs, and the moon is plenty watery already! Align with your intuition, authenticity, emotional depth, and ideal life flow with a daylong celebration of water under the Pisces Full Moon. Wear or carry a moonstone. If possible, visit a natural body of water. At home, play music or white noise containing water sounds, or employ an indoor fountain. Light white candles in your bathroom, and take a shower or long sea salt bath. Create a small water altar with items such as seashells, water in a vase or glass, river rocks, or mermaid pictures. And, when the moon is out, sit outside in quiet contemplation as you gaze at it. Hold a glass of water up to the moonlight and say:

Watery moon, hail and welcome! I call down your fluid receptivity and magical depths. With love, I drink to you and align myself with you. Thank you.

Tess Whitehurst

August 30

Sunday

3rd ♓

Color of the day: Yellow
Incense of the day: Frankincense

Personal Deity

Most of us call upon specific goddesses and gods who have deep meaning to us. It is unfortunate, but this world remains less welcoming to those of Pagan persuasion. Our earth-based belief systems often remain private and unspoken due to concerns about family or employers.

What can you do when you wish to include a symbol of your faith in an open environment, such as on a kitchen shelf or your desk? My personal goddess is Io. Loved by Zeus, forced to change into a cow, tortured by Hera—Io eventually was made human again and honored in her lifetime. The Ionian Sea is named for her. Her gem is iolite, a lustrous dark blue stone. I have a whimsical little statue of a black and white cow, in a dress, holding a basket of wheat (symbol of abundance), with wheat all about her feet. This symbolic statue of Io, found in a thrift store, is innocent enough to be placed in plain sight.

Today is the start of the last week of summer for many in the Northern Hemisphere. Visit some of your local thrift or gift shops and seek out a representation of your patron deity or spirit guide or a symbol of abundance. Before purchasing an item, remember to gently blow away all former energies from it with your breath. A formal cleansing may be performed later. Say:

[Insert name here], I honor you with this symbol.

Guide me always. I delight in your protection.

Emyme

Notes:

August 31

Monday

3rd ♓

☽ v/c 2:53 am

☽ → ♈ 4:33 am

Color of the day: Gray

Incense of the day: Narcissus

A Druidic Invisibility Spell

The ancient Druids used plants for many purposes, including food, clothing, medicine, worship, and spellcraft. Fern symbolizes magic, discretion, and shelter. Because ferns grow in difficult places, they also represent people who have survived hardship. They are also easily overlooked. The Druids used fern to convey invisibility, or more precisely, the ability to pass without notice.

For this spell, you'll need a dried fern leaflet, gray thread, and two small pieces of smoked glass. A pair of melted marbles with a smoky or mirrored coating will work well too. Press the fern between the glass and bind it thoroughly with gray thread. Then say:

Fern underfoot, fern under glen,

Safe I go out, safe home again.

No one to look, nothing to see

But smoke and leaves—surely not me.

Carry the charm with you when you need to pass by hostile places or people in peace.

Elizabeth Barrette

September

September is the ninth month of the year. Its name is derived from the Latin word *septum*, which means "seventh," as it was the seventh month of the Roman calendar. Its astrological sign is Virgo the maiden (August 23–September 23), a mutable earth sign ruled by Mercury. September is the dreamy golden afternoon of the year. Summer thins away, but September is a treasure chest filled with bounty and color. Apples ripen in the orchards. Purple grapes are harvested, and yellow heads of goldenrod nod along the roadsides. At Mabon, we celebrate the autumn equinox, and the dual nature of life/death. Now we're reminded of the goddess Demeter, and how her period of mourning for her abducted daughter Persephone coincides with nature's decline. To honor Demeter, drape your altar with purple fabric, and upon it place one red apple. Meditate about what you have and what you wish for. Bury the apple as you visualize your wish coming true. By September's end, autumn's flame begins to burn. You can see it in the orange of the maples and in the purple wild asters. Golden September—it's a time to dream, and a time to make those dreams come true.

James Kambos

September 1
Tuesday

3rd ♈

☽ v/c 12:37 pm

Color of the day: Red
Incense of the day: Bayberry

School Supplies

It's said that the sense of smell is our most powerful sensory ally. In the fall, the excitement of the new school year comes with scents of school bus–yellow pencils, new crayons, dry paper, and rubbery pink pearl erasers.

Recapture the energy and new beginnings of the school season with your own school supplies. Head to the local office supply store and purchase a composition book, pencils, crayons, and an eraser. Once home, play with your new school supplies, embracing them with all of your senses. Seize the chance to make a fresh start, perhaps writing, sketching, or embarking on a course of study. Enter the starting date into your composition book, anchoring it with a sigil of your own creation. Make a plan and set some goals; each time you sit down to work, chant:

Motivation, inspiration,
perspiration, exaltation!

Susan Pesznecker

September 2
Wednesday

3rd ♈

☽ → ♉ 5:02 am

Color of the day: White
Incense of the day: Honeysuckle

Less Stress

Aromatherapy calms the mind as well as the body when used to help reduce stress in our lives. I like to keep small Mason/jelly jars (four-ounce size) around the house flavored with different scents.

I use a base mix of sea salt and Epson salt, adding my favorite essential oils. I prefer essential oils that are cold-pressed and pure, as I will be inhaling these vapors. Also, should I decide to use this as a scrub in the bath, these are not harmful to my skin. I like lavender, mint, clary sage, patchouli, citrus scents, and light floral for my mixes, but you know best your favorite scents and allergies. Add ten drops of oil to the top of the salt, then cover the jar and shake. Close up the jar when you leave the room. Add more oils when it gets weak. Experiment and make your own personal blends.

Boudica

September 3
Thursday

3rd ♉

Color of the day: Turquoise
Incense of the day: Nutmeg

Blackberry Pie Abundance Spell

The blackberry is a marvelous fruit. Low in sugar, it is easy to grow or find, and every part of the plant is useful. Tea made from blackberry leaves soothes a sick stomach, the roots have been used as an astringent, and the fruit can be eaten and used to dye cloth.

Magically, blackberries bring abundance, good health, and protection. Bring these qualities into your life by preparing your favorite blackberry recipe—and infusing each step of the process with the words of this spell:

Dark and sweet

And good to eat.

Bring good health

And abundant wealth.

Blessed blackberry!

If possible, pick your own fruit so you can whisper the incantation into each berry as you select it. Repeat the spell as you gather your fruit, prepare your recipe, and serve it. Enjoy the fruits of your labor—literally—as you ingest blackberry's magical properties.

Natalie Zaman

September 4
Friday

3rd ♉

☽ v/c 6:20 am

☽ → ♊ 7:48 am

Color of the day: Pink
Incense of the day: Vanilla

The Boys of Fall Spell

It's my favorite season—football season. If you have a loved one who plays football, here's a protection spell to try. Place a photo of your football player—in uniform, of course—on your altar. For this spell, you'll invoke Mars, the warrior god and protector of athletes, so have some items on your altar associated with him. This could be things such as a photo of a wolf or a rooster. Have the altar decorated with a red candle and chrysanthemums for protection. Also include a small dish of ground ginger.

Place the photo before the candle, then light the candle. As the flame grows, see a ring of protection surrounding the photo. Sprinkle the ginger around the photo and say:

Mars, warrior and protector,

Hear this charm.

Protect [Name],

And keep [him/her] safe from harm.

Snuff out the candle, but don't move the photo until after the game.

James Kambos

September 5

Saturday

3rd ♊
4th Quarter 5:54 am
☽ v/c 7:04 pm

Color of the day: Gray
Incense of the day: Magnolia

Spell to Make a Difference

On this day in 1997, Nobel Peace Prize winner Mother Teresa died. Although Catholic, she was widely known and revered by people of many faiths around the world. Mother Teresa was noted for her goals and intentions to assist the sick and the poor.

On this day, no matter what our personal financial or health status, we can contemplate how we ourselves may be able to better assist those in need around us in some way. Find a white or purple candle and a safe holder and a favorite healing anointing oil, such as lavender. Anoint the candle with the intention of illuminating in your consciousness ways that you can assist others in need from the place you are in life today. Light the candle, and in meditation, envision its radiant light bringing clarity, inspiration, and illumination.

Blake Octavian Blair

 September 6

Sunday

4th ♊
☽ → ♋ 1:40 pm

Color of the day: Gold
Incense of the day: Hyacinth

Fight Procrastination Day

Today is Fight Procrastination Day. You need to replenish your supplies. You need to change out your altar cloth. You need to wash up all the jars and pots and candle holders. You need to prepare for the coming change in the Wheel of the Year. Summer is over, and fall is around the corner. Well, what are you waiting for?

Today is the day to really get down and accomplish something. Do not leave it undone. At least make a start on one project.

Call upon your personal totem, spirit animal, god, or goddess to push you along. Offer up this little spell and jump into the day's work:

No longer will I put off
Work large and small.
At chores I will not scoff,
I will accomplish them all.

Emyme

September 7

Monday

4th ♋

Color of the day: White
Incense of the day: Neroli

Labor Day

Will the World Civil Rights

Print, bless, and then distribute ninety-three copies of the Bill of Rights today in an effort to help manifest global change. Roll them up individually, and bind each copy with a single red ribbon to symbolize the loving limitlessness of Our Lady of Babylon.

Bless each roll with frankincense and myrrh incense. As you do so, recite the following Thelemic oath to devote to humanitarian peace and civil rights. This excerpt is found in *The Book of Thoth* and was written by Aleister Crowley as an oath written during the Dawn-Meditation. Used by aspiring occultists to comprehend a singular purpose, or Great Work, it is an essential gnostic step as a life-path coagulates beneath the feet. Crowley told us in *The Law Is for All:*

In his absolute innocence and ignorance Aiwass is The Fool; he is the Saviour, being the Son [Horus] who shall trample on the crocodiles and tigers, and avenge his father Osiris.

Most, bridal bound, my quintessential Form thus freeing from self, be found one Selfhood bent in Spirit-Being.

Estha McNevin

Notes:

September 8

Tuesday

4th ♋

☽ v/c 9:28 pm

☽ → ♌ 10:36 pm

Color of the day: Gray
Incense of the day: Basil

Singing and Vocal Intonation

Music of some variety is sacred to virtually all cultures worldwide. Many believe that the most sacred instrument is the human voice, it being our gods-given instrument.

Think about the intention you wish to manifest. Rather than creating a spell or ritual in the usual manner, try creating one using only your voice. Write songs to the elements and to the gods, and sing your spellcraft through the ceremony. Vow to only use your singing voice for the duration of the ritual. When utilizing words of power, chant these in long, sustained notes of deep vibration. Consider using musical instruments in the rite.

For added inspiration, carve the alchemical symbol of the planet Mercury (☿) on a yellow candle. Add some musical notes, and burn the candle during ritual as a declaration to the gods of sound. Additionally, because of the associations with the air element (which rules vocals, thought, and instrumentation), consider burning heavy clouds of incense while you perform the ceremony. Most of all, have fun!

Raven Digitalis

Notes:

September 9
Wednesday

4th ♌

Color of the day: Yellow
Incense of the day: Marjoram

Where'd I Leave It?

Ever misplace something and you know it's there somewhere, but for the life of you, you just can't find it? This spell may be just the thing to help.

You will need a pendulum, or something to act as a pendulum. Stand in the center of the room in which you think the lost item might be hiding, and do your best to still yourself. Say to yourself something along the lines of:

> *[Lost item], come to me,*
> *come to me, come to me.*

Note in which direction the pendulum swings the strongest. Move in that direction and repeat the question. Keep moving and chanting until it is no longer feasible to do so, then stop and search the area indicated. The places in which to look should be narrowed down quite a bit.

Laurel Reufner

 ## September 10
Thursday

4th ♌

Color of the day: Crimson
Incense of the day: Apricot

Balsamic Moon Dream Pillow

The final phase of the moon, just before the dark/new moon, is known as the balsamic moon. This is a time for rest and recuperation. It is also a good time for dreamwork. A nice herbal blend for a prophetic dream pillow is to mix one part mugwort, one part mullein, and ½ part vetivert, sewn into a black pillowcase. You can sleep on this not only to help encourage prophetic dreams but also to help ward off nightmares.

If you wish, you can turn the herb blend into an oil by converting the parts into teaspoons and adding the herbs to ½ cup vegetable oil. Simmer in a pot over very low heat until you can smell the herbs in the air, then remove from heat and allow to cool. Once the oil is cooled, strain and bottle it for use.

Michael Furie

September 11

Friday

4th ♌

☽ v/c 9:03 am

☽ → ♍ 9:56 am

Color of the day: Rose
Incense of the day: Yarrow

Make Room for Beauty

Magical folk love to beautify—our homes, our bodies, and our lives. Beauty in and of itself attracts positivity, as demonstrated by the synonym "attractiveness." Today, make room for sparkling beauty and the attraction of all good things by lighting a pink candle and calling on a deity who specializes in beauty, such as Archangel Jophiel, Venus, Aphrodite, Hathor, or Lakshmi. Say:

_____, I am your devotee, and I am a devotee of beauty! Please help me as I clear out the old and make room for the new. Thank you.

Then begin clearing clutter related to all forms of aesthetics. For example, get rid of old and unloved beauty products and tools, toiletries, home décor, art supplies, clothing, accessories, and non-beautifying foods. As a result of your effort, you will find that in the coming weeks and months, beautiful items and conditions will flow into your life more abundantly.

Tess Whitehurst

 September 12

Saturday

4th ♍

Color of the day: Blue
Incense of the day: Pine

Sacred Dreaming Spell

As we move closer to autumn, it's time to think about the dream realm and all it can offer to our personal pathwork. Find a space in your bedroom where you can set up an altar to dreaming, and decorate it with deep blues and silver, making sure to leave space for a notebook, a pen, and a white, blue, or silver candle. You may wish to make a dream pillow, but don't overstuff it! You want it to be comfortable to sleep upon. Good herbs to use are lavender, rose, mugwort, lemon, and sandalwood.

Take a bath or shower before bed to cleanse and purify yourself from your day. Light your candle and say prayers to your chosen deity for the kind of dream you wish to have. While falling asleep, focus on the fact that the answers are coming to you now, and try not to let your mind fall into the mundane. When you awaken, write down the dream immediately, and act upon the advice given.

Thuri Calafia

September 13

Sunday

4th ♏

New Moon 2:41 am

☽ v/c 10:08 pm

☽ → ♎ 10:41 pm

Color of the day: Orange
Incense of the day: Frankincense

Solar Eclipse

Sandalwood Journey Spell

Sandalwood comes from the heart of a tree and exudes a sweet scent. It conveys protection, security, and calm. It banishes evil. People often use this material in spells for safe travel.

For this spell, you will need a sandalwood bead and three white candles. (If you can't find a sandalwood bead, use any wooden bead anointed with sandalwood oil instead.) Place the bead inside a triangle of white candles. Light the wicks, then say:

Sandalwood, so sweet and strong,

Guard me on my journey long.

Guide me safely as I roam,

'Til I make my way back home.

Let the candles burn down in a safe place. Wear the bead in your hair or carry it while you travel. You may cast this spell with extra beads for more people or for your luggage.

Elizabeth Barrette

September 14

Monday

1st ♎

Color of the day: Gray
Incense of the day: Lily

Rosh Hashanah

An Apple Prosperity Spell

Apples are in season, so here's a prosperity spell you can really sink your teeth into.

Find a nice red apple and wash it. Dry it with a green cloth. Then really rub it hard. As you rub it, keep thinking of wealth coming to you. Hold the apple before you and say this charm:

With this apple so red, this spell is fed.

Bring me the money I need.

Next, slice the apple in two. With a sharp knife, cut the shape of a dollar sign into the skin of one half and set aside. Eat the other half. End the spell by burying the half that is decorated with the dollar sign as a gesture of thanks. Try not to think anymore about the spell once you bury the apple half.

James Kambos

September 15

Tuesday

1st ♎︎

Color of the day: White
Incense of the day: Ginger

Respect for the Aged Day

This is a national holiday in Japan to honor elderly people. Japan has the world's longest life expectancy, and the wisdom of the elders is highly regarded. On this day, they are appreciated for their contributions to society, and their presence is valued in the home and the entire community. Use today to honor the elders in your life, and take a moment to realize that someday you will be among that group.

Amulets to protect the wearer are commonly given on this day. In addition, you may wish to make one of these for an elderly person in your life (or yourself). Mix dried mullein, a dried peach pit or wood from a peach tree, and dried vervain in a white or red bag. These herbs are traditionally used to promote longevity, youth, and health. Carry the pouch with you or give it as a gift.

Ember Grant

 September 16

Wednesday

1st ♎︎

☽ v/c 12:22 am
☽ → ♏︎ 11:43 am

Color of the day: Topaz
Incense of the day: Lilac

Make a Floral Carpet

Onam is a Hindu harvest festival with mythological overtones. People celebrate with music, dancing, and feasts. A pookalam, or floral carpet, is made by arranging masses of flower petals into a design like a mandala. A clay statue of the deity Vamana may be placed within or beside the pookalam. The feasts feature curries, pickles, and rice.

Honor this holiday by making a floral carpet of your own. You may choose tropical flowers from India, or local ones in season such as aster, chrysanthemum, daisy, rose, sunflower, and zinnia. Use color and floral correspondences to symbolize what you desire, such as a fruitful harvest, a beautiful landscape, a tranquil home, or a healthy nation. Pull the petals off the flower heads and use them to make an attractive design. As you work, concentrate on what you want to manifest.

Afterward, take a photo of your pookalam to save and remember later.

Elizabeth Barrette

♃eptember 17

Thursday

1st ♏

Color of the day: Purple
Incense of the day: Mulberry

Witchy Window Hex Charms

As the trees begin to display nature's opulent death, windows that were once sheltered by lush foliage can become barren and exposed by the season's overture of repose. Simple hex signs like eyes, crosses, seven-pointed stars, and trinity knots seal the fortunes and prosperity of the family into the very fibers of the home. These traditional protective symbols are often painted and written on glass windows using wax and watercolor crayons, or are soldered together into their various shapes, as is the case with stained glass. This magic of intentional rampart fortification goes a long way toward protecting us from unwanted dangers by reinforcing all portals in and out of the home.

Distribute any or all of these symbols upon each door and window from the inside. It is up to you how large or small you make them. As you draw each symbol, envision it glowing as a ward against all passing energy preset to harm. Focus all of your energy and movements into channeling this sense of total safety and protection. Wash your windows every season, and repeat this spell as needed.

Estha McNevin

Notes:

September 18

Friday

1st ♏

☽ v/c 3:49 pm

☽ → ♐ 11:32 pm

Color of the day: Coral
Incense of the day: Orchid

The Healthy Body Beauty Spell

Beauty is only skin deep, so some say, but real beauty comes from within.

Treating yourself well is a good start toward a healthy body. Nutritious foods, lots of water, fresh air, and sunshine are starters. Get out and get physical to keep your whole body healthy. Be sure to see the doctor once a year to keep that body in perfect running condition.

Feed your mind good books, and keep your inner child fed with entertainment. You can also find study courses for free from well-known learning institutions online.

Finally, feed the soul. Spend some time nurturing your spirituality. I recommend doing this daily, but once a week can be a start. A simple meditation for a couple of minutes can restore some inner peace, and it can help relieve that stress you feel at the end of the day.

Take care of the things that matter, and your inner beauty will shine through.

Boudica

 September 19

Saturday

1st ♐

Color of the day: Black
Incense of the day: Sage

Talk Like a Pirate Day

Talk Like a Pirate Day is celebrated every September 19th. Begun as a joke among friends, this fanciful idea quickly took off after it was highlighted in a national newspaper column. Last year, did you remember to dig up any treasure you buried in 2013? If not, get out that shovel. Many holidays start as someone's creative idea, take hold, and evolve into something worthwhile. Historically, some pirates were actually privateers contracted by governments to put the destructive pirates out of business.

Today, call upon your inner pirate and plunder. Scour your home for booty for which you no longer have use and donate it to a local charity. Or delve into your treasure chest and donate a sum to a local animal shelter in the name of your trusty parrot companion. You may wish to have friends and family over and make it a group effort in order to donate a larger amount. Plan a neighborhood "treasure hunt" ending at your home. Include rum punch with your cakes and ale. Aarrghh!

Emyme

September 20

Sunday

1st ♍ ♐

Color of the day: Yellow
Incense of the day: Heliotrope

Spell to Encourage a Legal Victory

If you want to encourage victory in a legal dispute, here is a great option. This spell avoids problems by using a bloodstone, which can be carried without inciting alarm (no metal or herbs). First, create an oil by simmering one tablespoon Alpinia galangal (greater galangal, or "court case root") and one tablespoon black mustard seeds in ½ cup sunflower oil for three minutes, then cool, strain, and bottle. Anoint a brown candle for justice with the oil (placing it on the left of your altar) and a purple candle for power (placing it on the right).

Set the tarot card Justice between the candles, placing the bloodstone on it. Light the candles and hold your hands over the bloodstone, saying this spell:

Scales of justice, tip my way.

Defeat opponents that I face.

My wishes shall carry the day.

Battle ended; I win my case!

Michael Furie

September 21

Monday

1st ♐

☽ v/c 4:59 am

2nd Quarter 4:59 am

☽ → ♑ 8:33 am

Color of the day: Silver
Incense of the day: Narcissus

UN International Day of Peace

Spell for Peace and Understanding

Today is the UN International Day of Peace. Conflict between both individuals and nations is often rooted in misunderstanding. It is true that we often fear that which we do not understand. In the spirit of understanding through knowledge and education, pick a person you are having a conflict with and make a civil attempt to talk with them and learn more about where they are coming from in their stance. Or perhaps pick a nation that your country is in conflict with, and learn more about its people, history, and culture. Attempt to set aside and dispel preconceived notions or misconceptions you have about them.

Next, charge two candles. One candle represents you or your nation, and the other represents the person or nation the conflict is with. Light the candles with the intent for healing and understanding for both parties.

Envision the light surrounding all involved. Let the candles burn out safely.

Blake Octavian Blair

NOTES:

September 22

Tuesday

2nd ♑

☽ v/c 7:13 pm

Color of the day: Maroon
Incense of the day: Cedar

Air head

The element of air is associated with clarity and thought, which are useful during periods of change (like the seasonal conversion that's happening tomorrow). Go for an autumn walk and look for feathers—nature's own wand of air that, charged with your energy, will engage this element to help you think clearly.

Clean the feather, first to remove any physical dirt and then with saltwater to remove any lingering energies. Blow on the feather—this will dry it and imprint it with your energy. Whenever your mind feels muddled, take your feather and, holding it level with your chin, pass it over your face and brow, then over the top of your head and down the back, and say:

Feathery wand of sylph and air,

Clear my head, sweep away care!

Visualize any cloudiness being pulled back like a veil. Think or repeat the spell whenever you need to clear your mind.

Natalie Zaman

NOTES:

September 23

Wednesday

2nd ♑

☉ → ♎ 4:21 am

☽ → ♒ 1:51 pm

Color of the day: Brown
Incense of the day: Lavender

Mabon – Fall Equinox – Yom Kippur

The Fall Equinox

Mabon is the major harvest festival on the seasonal Wheel of the Year. It's also known as the fall or autumnal equinox and, in folk terms, as "harvest home." Astrologically, Mabon occurs when the Sun enters Libra, balancing night and day equally. It is the halfway point between summer and winter and a time of joy, sorrow, and change as days grow shorter and winter advances. Plants wither and die, trees drop their leaves, and the first frosts arrive. We mourn the passing of light but celebrate the harvest, aware that life's Wheel has turned again. There are no ends, nor beginnings—only the spiraling continuance of life eternal.

In the Scottish highlands, the cutting of the last sheaf of wheat means the falling of the harvest spirits. The final bit of wheat is braided into a "corn dolly" effigy and featured prominently in communal celebration. The party ends with the effigy being buried in the empty fields, a symbolic sacrifice to ensure the fertility of the lands in the coming year.

Make your own corn dolly and bury it in your garden, beseeching the lands for fertility and success:

The trees are standing bare,

And the wheat is bending down.

May fortune smile down upon

This blessed sacred ground.

Susan Pesznecker

NOTES:

September 24

Thursday

2nd ♒︎

Color of the day: White
Incense of the day: Jasmine

Kubera Mudra

The Kubera mudra is dedicated to the god of wealth, Kubera. Use it for pursuing your goals or wishes. It can bring more than just prosperity. Mentally it grants confidence, serenity, and inner poise. Physically it aids decongestion and other opening effects. Also known as the Three-Finger Technique, this mudra aids in finding something specific, such as a book in a library or an open parking space on a street.

First touch together the tips of your thumb, index finger, and middle finger. Then curl your ring finger and little finger so they touch your palm. Frame your goal into words, using a positive perspective. Speak it aloud three times as you press your fingertips together.

Imagine that your desire has already manifested, and concentrate on how you will enjoy it. This present focus helps bring your wishes to fruition.

Elizabeth Barrette

▽ September 25

Friday

2nd ♒︎
☽ v/c 12:02 am
☽ → ♓︎ 3:43 pm

Color of the day: Purple
Incense of the day: Rose

Tree-hugging hippie Magick

Even if Pagans are dubbed "tree-hugging hippies" from time to time, it's not really that insulting. Since Pagans worship and adore nature, and we ideally make choices every day that support this alignment, you may wish to try this simple spell that utilizes the raw forces of nature.

Simply go to a favorite tree in your area, or take a walk in a wooded area and find one you feel a kinship with. Hug the tree for a few minutes. Kiss the wood and whisper your prayers into its mighty base. Feel yourself merging with its incredible power. Declare your alignment to Mother Earth, and ask for protection through your days. Be sure to leave an offering of a fruit, vegetable, or grain. Return to the tree and repeat the process whenever you're in need of mental grounding and the potent protection of the Great Mother.

Vow to always make life choices that benefit the earth, including recycling, eating locally, and supporting small businesses.

Raven Digitalis

September 26

Saturday

2nd ♓

☽ v/c 12:32 pm

Color of the day: Indigo
Incense of the day: Patchouli

Solitary Tea Ceremony

A Japanese tea ceremony, from start to finish, is a meditation on simplicity and present moment awareness. Perform a simplified tea ceremony with just one guest: you. Before you begin, focus on your breath. Feel your weight on the floor. Listen to the sounds around you. Really be present. Then continue to breathe consciously as you brew yourself a cup of your favorite tea. Lovingly choose a cup, attentively appreciate the rising steam, and notice the subtle botanical scent. When it's prepared to your liking, sit comfortably and drink, paying close attention to the taste in your mouth and the warm feeling in your throat and belly. When you notice your mind wandering, just smile to yourself and come back to the moment. And whenever anything arises, internally or externally, say "yes" to it. Love and embrace your-self—and all your actions, thoughts, strengths, and challenges—exactly as you are.

Tess Whitehurst

 September 27

Sunday

2nd ♓

☽ → ♈ 3:29 pm

Full Moon 10:51 pm

Color of the day: Amber
Incense of the day: Eucalyptus

Lunar Eclipse

Motivational Moon Magic

A ll too often, it's really hard to get going on that project or report. If only we could just get started, then everything would be fine. Spend some time tonight har-nessing the potential energy bursting from the full moon, which you can then draw upon when you need an extra push to get going.

Fill a small decorative bottle with moving water from somewhere that has meaning for you. I like to use ocean water, because it's filled with so much primordial potential, but any water will do. In the light of the full moon, drop red candle wax around the top of the bottle, then allow the bottle to continue to sit in the moonlight, soaking up the energy in the moonbeams. Pull the bottle out and set it nearby when you need that extra bit of energy and willpower to get to work.

Laurel Reufner

September 28
Monday

3rd ♈

Color of the day: Ivory
Incense of the day: Rosemary

Sukkot begins

Rulership over Yourself

In classical Rome, this day was devoted to the Capitoline Triad—Jupiter, Juno, and Minerva—who are believed to have originally been Etruscan deities. The Triad were the divine protectors of the state and spoke via auguries. If we think of these deities as ruling body, soul, and mind, we can perhaps get some auguries for ourselves today.

Select the Empress, Emperor, and Strength cards from your favorite tarot deck and lay them on your altar. Place a quartz crystal, holey stone, or other significant stone on each card to magnify what each deity says to you. Light purple or indigo candles, and go into your alpha state. Engage in conversation with these deities. Ask Jupiter what you can do to improve or preserve your physical health. Ask Juno about your spiritual and emotional health. Ask Minerva about your mental health. If their advice seems to be sound, follow it.

Barbara Ardinger, PhD

 ## September 29
Tuesday

3rd ♈

☽ v/c 3:45 am
☽ → ♉ 2:57 pm

Color of the day: Black
Incense of the day: Cinnamon

Water Elemental Spell

With Mercury in retrograde, intuition and instinct work better than words or phrases. Take a moment under this barely waning moon, and meditate on the energies of water, its ability to wear away mountains, to cleanse, and to heal. See whirlpools and waves, rivers and waterfalls in your mind. Feel the cool, clean, silky texture of its liquid power with your psychic senses. Know that this is the path of the emotions, and that feelings are neither right nor wrong—they just are. Open to the energies of water, experience them, let them fill and heal you. Breathe deeply, opening to the flow, the heart, and the deep cleansing and healing of your emotions, and promise yourself that you will honor your emotions by being true to them from this day forward. Blessed be.

Thuri Calafia

September 30
Wednesday

3rd ♉

Color of the day: White
Incense of the day: Bay laurel

Opportunity Spell

Even if you're satisfied with your current job, use this spell to achieve added success or increase your performance. If you're searching for a job, this spell can help you find one that's right for you. It's important to keep an open mind, even if you have your eye on the ideal job. Remember to actively pursue all opportunities.

Place one green candle and one orange candle together in a large dish or bowl. Sprinkle sage around the candles. Visualize your intent as you light the candles and invoke Janus, god of beginnings, for a literal new beginning or to approach your existing job with a new perspective. Chant:

Bring me what I need

In order to succeed.

Strength to know and build

And keep my life fulfilled.

Ember Grant

NOTES:

October

October is a busy month. Originally the eighth month of the year (*octo* being eight) in the Roman calendar, it was set back to the tenth month around 700 BCE, when King Numa Pompilius revised the calendar and added January and February.

The ancient Egyptians celebrate the Festival of Het-Hert, or Hathor, on October 4th. The Romans celebrate Meditrinalia on October 11th, tasting the new wine for the first time and honoring Jupiter as god of the wine. And the Celts close out their year at Samhain on October 31st.

In October, we are most aware of the shortening of the days, the cooling weather, the changing colors of the trees and the falling of the leaves, glowing fires, orange pumpkins, and warm scarves and mittens.

The last of the harvest festivals arrives at Halloween. The veil thins, and we feel the presence of our ancestors and those we cherish who have passed over. We set a place at the table for them and celebrate with them the passing of another season and the closing of another year.

The larders are full against the coming winter months. The last mornings of October bring the killing frosts, and we wait prepared for the change in season yet to come.

Boudica

October 1
Thursday

3rd ♉

☽ v/c 6:44 am

☽ → ♊ 4:03 pm

Color of the day: Green
Incense of the day: Carnation

Re-creating Seawater

The ocean is a powerful source of magic and energy. It features in mythology around the world. It embodies the divine feminine. The ocean symbolizes mystery, mysticism, and power. Therefore, seawater functions in many spells. This poses a challenge for people who live inland.

You can make your own seawater for ritual use. For this, you will need distilled water and sea salt. You can find sea salt for the kitchen at natural food stores, or you can get the kind meant for saltwater aquariums at a pet store, which has a formula on the back. A good rule of thumb is about half a cup of salt per gallon of water. Add a blessing if you wish.

Set the container of water outdoors or in a window for twenty-four hours, exposing it to sunlight and moonlight. After this, you can use it in spells or rituals.

Elizabeth Barrette

October 2
Friday

3rd ♊

Color of the day: Rose
Incense of the day: Mint

honoring Guardian Spirits

Today, the Catholic Church observes the Feast of the Guardian Angels. However, angels are not restricted to Christianity. Angels appear across cultures and spiritualities in many forms and predate Christianity. Although many of us already do so daily, take a few extra minutes today to honor your personal guardian spirits, whatever their form may be for you. It could be an angel, saint, patron god or goddess, power animal, ancestor, or other spirit. The relationship between a practitioner and his or her guardian spirits is one where reciprocity and teamwork factor heavily. In honor of the reciprocity for the guidance and protection you receive in your relationship with your guardian spirits, make an offering to them of something they enjoy, and light a candle to them on your altar. Voice your gratitude to them:

Gratitude and honor for the relationship between you and me.

For your protection and guidance, I thank thee!

Blake Octavian Blair

October 3

Saturday

3rd ♊

☽ v/c 1:18 pm

☽ → ♋ 8:22 pm

Color of the day: Indigo

Incense of the day: Sandalwood

Break a Curse Spell

To destroy a curse, cast this spell at midnight. You'll need a fire in a fireplace, preferably; a cauldron will do. Gather three twigs, one each of oak, pine, and ash. Build a fire, but don't burn the twigs yet. Gazing at the flames, say:

Fire, destroy the curse.

Its power I will reverse.

Twigs of oak, pine, and ash

Shall make the curse a thing of the past.

Lay the twigs upon the flames, and listen as they crackle and hiss. Say:

Wood, burn, to the sender the curse shall return.

Now angrily spit into the fire three times, and say with all your heart:

Sacred wood, consumed by firelight,

Thank you for your help tonight.

I thank the guardians of east, west, north, and south.

May this curse die within the fire's mouth!

Let the ashes cool for seven days, then scatter them to the wind. As you do so, laugh!

James Kambos

Notes:

October 4
Sunday

3rd ♋
4th Quarter 5:06 pm

Color of the day: Amber
Incense of the day: Almond

Sukkot ends

Living Earth

Of the four cardinal elements, earth is the most foundational. The planet Earth is our home, and the earth element is the bedrock that provides stability to our lives and keeps our feet, physically and metaphorically, on the ground.

Spend a day (or longer) focusing deeply on your connection to the earth element. Dress in natural fibers and colors, and go barefoot if you're able to. Carry obsidian, malachite, and turquoise in your pockets—stones powerfully associated with earth and grounding. Taking a lawn chair, a blanket or umbrella (if needed), and a copy of one of Henry David Thoreau's or John Muir's works, go to a quiet outdoor location and sit quietly, becoming familiar with the place and letting its scents, sounds, and sights slip into you. Read from your book, feeling the connection with Earth and earth. Speak aloud:

Earth, I am your protector.

Susan Pesznecker

October 5
Monday

4th ♋
☽ v/c 7:04 am

Color of the day: White
Incense of the day: Hyssop

World Teachers' Day

In these economically stressed times, schools and teachers need all the help they can get. I recently heard a parent complain about having to cover her child's soft-cover and paperback books with clear plastic contact paper. Although plastic may strike some as being not ecologically sound, books do need to be protected. When I was in school, we used brown paper grocery bags or craft paper. These days there are "book sox," stretchy cloth covers. Neither of these options may work very well on paperback books.

Whatever your choice or option, make a ritual out of honoring the written word. It is refreshing that schools continue to provide books to students.

Gather your supplies and light a candle. Ground and center. Another possibility is to use this occasion to encourage children to create their first grimoire. Say:

Athena/Minerva, bless this activity.
We cover and protect books.
We honor the written word.

We respect the lessons within.
Inspire us and guide us to use these
to the best of our abilities.

Emyme

NOTES:

October 6

Tuesday

4th ♋

☽ → ♌ 4:31 am

Color of the day: Gray
Incense of the day: Bayberry

healing Body Soak

For this spell, assemble:

- Three cups Epsom salt, to draw out impurities

- Three tablespoons mustard powder, to warm the bones

- One tablespoon bishop's weed, crushed to heal the flesh

- One tablespoon thyme, to restore vigor

- Three drops frankincense essential oil, to battle evil

- One drop oregano essential oil, to heal disease

- One drop lemongrass essential oil, to banish pain

Combine all of the ingredients into a salt blend. Draw a sacred bath by first thoroughly scrubbing the tub, then salting and rinsing it before filling. Steep the ingredients for five minutes and then climb in the bath. As you soak, move and flex your muscles and joints to feel them release in the warm water. Imagine all of your pain, illness, and disease rushing to exit your body, sweating out of your glands, and being released into the water.

When you feel renewed with vigor, drain the tub as you sit in the water. Feel the pull of gravity drawing illness away from you and down the drain. When the tub is empty, shower quickly in extremely hot water. Then crawl right into bed for a nap, and allow your body to sweat out the rest of the toxins and hibernate for self-healing.

When you awake, shower again, wash your bedding to remove all traces of illness, and engage in a stretching routine like yoga or tai chi to bolster the effect of this healing bath spell.

Estha McNevin

NOTES:

October 7
Wednesday

4th ♌
☽ v/c 5:10 pm

Color of the day: Yellow
Incense of the day: Honeysuckle

The Dragon Dance

Today is the first day of the festival known as Nagasaki Kunchi. Recognized by the colorful "Dragon Dance," its underpinnings—which originated in the 1600s—might be seen as the inverse of Saint Patrick "driving the snakes out of Ireland." The fiery, snake-like dragon makes his way through the festival, symbolically driving out the forbidden "hidden Christians," and promoting more traditional regional beliefs such as Shinto and Buddhism.

Although many of us now possess the unalienable right to choose our own spiritual path (unlike residents of medieval Ireland or of Nagasaki after its "Christian Period"), we can still harbor lingering negativity from harsh spiritual upbringings. Today, do your own dragon dance and drive lingering demons of fear-based spirituality out of your consciousness for good. Light red and orange candles, play festive music with a good beat, drape brightly colored scarves about your body, and dance, snake-like, with the spirit of freedom.

Tess Whitehurst

October 8
Thursday

4th ♌
☽ → ♍ 3:50 pm

Color of the day: Purple
Incense of the day: Myrhh

Increase Your Business

To increase business, use a seven-day Better Business candle anointed with Better Business oil. There are many blends on the market, so pick one that feels right to you. You can also do a success working using a yellow candle and Success oil.

A good addition to your working is to write in gold ink on a blank business check for abundance. Put your business name on the "Pay To" line, and fill the amount space with "$$$$$$." Do not limit your goal by putting in a specific dollar amount. In the date space, put the date by which you want to see this increase manifest. Sign the check "Law of Attraction." Place the check on your business altar. Renew the working whenever your business starts to slack off or you need an extra push in sales.

Boudica

October 9

Friday

4th ♍

☽ v/c 6:12 pm

Color of the day: Coral
Incense of the day: Alder

Leaf Divination

Walking through the woods while leaves fall from the trees is one of autumn's most magical treats. Trees have been a source of spiritual sustenance and symbolic divination for centuries. The leaves can also have messages for us.

Go to a place where you can walk under falling leaves. Catch them, or pick up ones you are attracted to. What messages do the colors of the leaves impart?

- Green = growth, abundance, luck, health

- Red = passion, love, strength, power

- Yellow = joy, hope, sunshine

- Brown = stability, comfort, home, simplicity

- Orange = energy, balance, enthusiasm, warmth

- Purple = spirituality, mystery, transformation, wisdom

Consider everything about each leaf to determine its message. Is it whole? Is it dry, or still fresh? What kind of tree did the leaf come from? Use your favorite reference about tree symbolism to determine what meaning the tree has for you.

Natalie Zaman

NOTES:

October 10

Saturday

4th ♏

Color of the day: Black
Incense of the day: Ivy

Reviving the Golden Age

Today is Saturday. Astrologers tell us that Saturn is associated with restrictions and limitations. Not necessarily. This early Roman god of planting and harvest was King of the Golden Age, an ancient era of peace, harmony, stability, and prosperity. We're living in the Iron Age today, but the news media keep reporting stories that make the world seem like it's fallen into a Leaden Age and is swiftly sinking deeper into an abyss of war and ignorance.

Let's help the world recover its lost golden qualities and climb back toward the Golden Age. Carry a gold coin in your wallet or pocket. Keep black tourmaline on your altar for grounding and centering, and agates for strength, courage, and healing. Wear turquoise for peace of mind, creativity, and intuition. Starting today, honor old King Saturn by actively following the Wiccan Rede. Practice loving-kindness and donate your time and money to worthy organizations.

Barbara Ardinger, PhD

 October 11

Sunday

4th ♏

☽ → ♎ 4:45 am

Color of the day: Yellow
Incense of the day: Marigold

Spell to Banish Wrongdoing

This spell banishes behavior patterns specific to a person who is no longer in your life. Gather together the petals of any flowers this person ever gave to you. If you don't have any, go outside and gather some colorful fallen leaves. Place them in a bowl on your altar. Make sure you ground and center well for this spell—you'll be using a lot of energy! Now, list all the energy patterns of the wrongdoing, ending with a banishing statement. For example, if this person damaged your self-esteem by shaming you, say:

I banish shaming! Shaming begone!

Use all the force you can muster to send this energy out of your home and your presence. When you're all finished, release the petals on the wind with these words:

I let you go in grace and bear you no ill will, but your negative energies are not welcome here.

Finally, charge the space with a favorite incense and a list of good energies you wish to invite into your home. Be blessed.

Thuri Calafia

October 12
Monday

4th ♎︎
☽ v/c 8:06 pm
🄽ew Moon 8:06 pm

Color of the day: Silver
Incense of the day: Clary sage

Columbus Day (observed)

Upcycled Protection

Several years ago, I found myself wondering what to do with my old herbs, as rosemary followed vervain into a bucket. Then the idea of creating a protective circle around our property hit me. This is a useful way to return the herbs to Mother Nature while adding an extra layer of protection to your home, and it works with any botanicals you might have on hand. Dump them all willy-nilly into a bucket or other container, and head outside. (You could even designate a container just for their collection and add to it over time as flowers die and herbs become dated.)

To create the circle, simply walk the perimeter of your property, clockwise if possible, strewing the herbs as you go. As you walk, envision a circle of protective white light flaring up around your home. Close the circle and it is done.

Laurel Reufner

October 13
Tuesday

1st ♎︎
☽ → ♏︎ 5:38 pm

Color of the day: Scarlet
Incense of the day: Ylang-ylang

Cemetery Spellcrafting

Find a peaceful cemetery in your area to visit. At dusk, bring an offering of herbs, alcohol (or juice), bread, fruit, or grain. Find an isolated area to be seated, and enter a state of somber, reflective meditation. You may choose to wear black and even a veil.

When the time is right, hold your offering high above your head and declare the following or something similar:

Oh great and powerful dead, I honor your life and understand my own mortality. I leave you this offering so that you may be at peace. May I be granted the same in my journey on earth as well as my journey after death. So mote it be.

Meditate on the energy of death. If you feel comfortable, consider performing some communication with the angel Azrael, he who oversees the life cycle. As per tradition, once you leave your offering in the cemetery, be sure not to look back as you leave.

Raven Digitalis

October 14
Wednesday

1st ♏

☽ v/c 8:58 pm

Color of the day: Brown
Incense of the day: Marjoram

Autumn Storage

This time of year signals the need to prepare for winter. It is time to take stock and begin to clean and put away the items used only in the summer. In modern times, this would include such things as lawnmowers and pool equipment. All of these things can be cleaned and stored with intent, bringing the magic of the everyday into your life.

For many of us, connecting to the seasonal shifts isn't really experienced through the planting or livestock cycles anymore. We do, however, have our own seasonal cycles, and we can use these to connect to the greater energy shifts of the earth. Even something as mundane as packing away swimsuits can be an opportunity to connect with the energy shift. Simply reminisce about summer and gradually shift focus to concentrate on the here and now, then visualize the coming winter.

Michael Furie

 October 15
Thursday

1st ♏

Color of the day: Green
Incense of the day: Apricot

Waxing Moon Bath

Bring a moonstone (or many moonstones) into the bath or shower with you (or wear moonstone jewelry). This spell draws upon the power of the waxing moon and is intended to increase your personal power. If you have a tub, put the stones in the water with you. Otherwise, wear them or place them nearby. Moonstones are associated with water and have strong feminine energy; combine all of these to supercharge your bath or shower and give your personal energy a magical boost. Light candles in the room as desired. While you wash, know that you're immersing yourself in moon-water. Repeat nightly through the full moon phase, if desired. Here's a chant you can use to help visualize the process:

Waxing moon, growing power,
water of the bath or shower,

Wash my body, touch my skin,
magic flowing out and in.

Ember Grant

October 16
Friday

1st ♏

☽ → ♐ 5:18 am

Color of the day: White
Incense of the day: Vanilla

Banish Sleep Inertia

Do you have trouble waking up in the morning? Do you feel as if you're still asleep for a while after getting out of bed? That feeling has a name: sleep inertia. Physically, it has to do with your body struggling to adjust its metabolic phase, especially if you're awakened from a deep sleep. Metaphysically, it's about your spirit settling back into your body after its nightly journeying to other planes.

To fight sleep inertia, first turn on bright lights. Hold a piece of onyx in your receptive (usually left) hand. Concentrate on grounding yourself fully in your body. Wiggle your toes and fingers a little. Then hold a piece of carnelian in your projective (usually right) hand. Focus on increasing your energy level. Stand up and move around. You may want to turn on lively music at this stage. Keep the stones by your bedside for use each morning.

Elizabeth Barrette

October 17
Saturday

1st ♐

Color of the day: Blue
Incense of the day: Rue

A Mirror Banishment Spell

Use this spell to remove a problem or a bad habit from your life. You'll need a small mirror, lipstick or a non-permanent marker, and some dried basil.

Sit at your altar and gaze at the mirror but don't look directly into it. Visualize your problem and how it affects you. Then see yourself free of this habit/problem. Do this for no more than ten minutes. Now write your problem on the mirror with the lipstick or marker. Lay the mirror on your altar, and sprinkle dried basil around it. Leave the mirror undisturbed overnight.

The next morning, discard the basil, and using soap and water, or window cleaner, wipe the writing off the mirror. Even after the mirror appears clean, continue rubbing it vigorously. Visualize your problem being wiped out of your life. When done, wrap your mirror in a light blue cloth and keep for other spells.

James Kambos

October 18
Sunday

1st ♐

☽ v/c 4:48 am

☽ → ♑ 2:52 pm

Color of the day: Orange
Incense of the day: Frankincense

Solar Peaceful Warrior Spell

Blessed Sun-day! Time for some solar magick in honor of today's planetary ruler. Many people have a powerful solar-aligned anointing oil in their kitchen and are totally unaware of it. Olive oil has potent alignments with the sun, masculinity, and the element of fire. Many associate such qualities with aggression, but they need not, especially when working with the powers of Olive, which is also associated with peace.

Today, using solar energy and the power of olive oil, let us light a candle in honor of walking the path of the peaceful warrior. Anoint a yellow candle with olive oil. Light it, and as you watch its radiant glow, recite the following:

By power of masculine sun,

Radiant, shining, fiery protective one,

And by peaceful power of Olive,

Powerful and certain progress can be won.

Gently and assertively along the road,

I shall proceed in this mode.

Blake Octavian Blair

NOTES:

October 19
Monday

1st ♍

Color of the day: Lavender
Incense of the day: Rosemary

Protect Your Furkid's Health and Well-Being

Most Pagans have furkids of some kind or another. You should know the name of the protector of your furkids. For cats, it is Bast. For dogs, it is Anubis.

Be sure that your pets see the vet regularly. The best medicine is prevention. If your animals are outdoor pets, be sure they have their rabies shots. Check for fleas regularly, and use a flea product to keep those nasty little bugs off your pet and out of your house. Be sure to have your outside pet spayed or neutered. And be sure to get a tracking chip.

But most of all, take care of your pets. Give them fresh water daily, feed them a balanced diet, and remember that junk food affects them much in the same way that it affects us. Take good care of your furkids, and the gods and goddesses will smile on their continued good health.

Boudica

October 20
Tuesday

1st ♍

☽ v/c 4:31 pm

2nd Quarter 4:31 pm

☽ → ♒ 9:38 pm

Color of the day: White
Incense of the day: Geranium

Apple Day

Apple Day is a celebration aimed at a region's terroir (terr-WAH), the special set of characteristics created by a region's weather, geology, geography, soil, and other natural conditions. Because of the wide diversity of apples and the way individual apple types are dependent upon terroir, they've come to be the center of this festivity.

Celebrate your own Apple Day by visiting a local orchard or your own apple trees, if you have any. Drink apple cider, bake an apple pie or cake, or stir up a batch of applesauce. If you have children, show them how to bob for apples.

Cut an apple in half around its equator, allowing the pentagram hidden inside to show. Lay one half at the base of an apple tree, offering blessings of thanks. Eat the other half next to the tree while you ground, center, and feel the connection to your own terroir.

Susan Pesznecker

October 21
Wednesday

2nd ♒

Color of the day: White
Incense of the day: Lilac

Midweek Mountain Grounding

Every Wednesday is a turning point—you're halfway through the week! Take a moment to recenter yourself with this mini version of Tadasana (Mountain Pose in yoga). Combined with a bit of visualization, you will feel reenergized and refreshed and ready to tackle the rest of the week.

Stand up straight and tall, and let your arms fall to your sides, palms open and turned toward your legs. Plant your feet firmly on the floor, the ball and heel first and then your toes. Feel yourself being supported by the ground beneath you. See yourself as a mountain, a part of the earth.

Now focus on your breath; close your eyes if you need to. Become aware of the rhythm as you inhale and exhale. Visualize that each breath out releases any stress, weariness, or negativity that you're feeling. With each breath in, see yourself taking in new, clean energy.

Repeat for ten inhalations/exhalations.

Natalie Zaman

 October 22
Thursday

2nd ♒

Color of the day: Turquoise
Incense of the day: Clove

Jidai Matsuri

Jidai Matsuri—or the Festival of the Ages—is celebrated today in Kyoto, Japan, with a parade, which begins with costumes and floats depicting the present era. Each successive wave symbolizes a more distant time period.

In the same spirit, gain perspective and bless your future with this ritual. Close your eyes and experience the present. Look at all the aspects of your life. Assess how you feel, where you are, and what you're working toward. Then move back in time ten years, and repeat. Repeat until you reach early childhood. Next, be your mother as an adult and similarly assess. Do the same with your father. Then be your mother at age five and perform the assessment. Then be your father at age five. Repeat with all four grandparents, and with as many generations as you like. Allow your imagination to fill in any details that you don't consciously know.

Tess Whitehurst

October 23

Friday

2nd ♒

☽ v/c 12:22 am

☽ → ♓ 1:18 am

☉ → ♏ 1:47 pm

Color of the day: Pink
Incense of the day: Violet

Light and Dark Waters

Create a magical light water to aid you in positive emotional workings, weddings, and spiritual attunements. Into a two-fluid-ounce bottle, carefully add a pinch of sea salt, slivers of selenite, freshwater pearls, and fluorite gravel. Fill this bottle with water from a sacred well. Use this water whenever you need the presence of light, peace, and protection.

Create a magical dark water to aid you in negative emotional release, banishing spells, and hex work. Into a two-fluid-ounce bottle, combine a pinch of black salt, charcoal slivers, and a jet stone. Fill this bottle with black water from a cesspool, pond, or swamp. Use this water whenever you need to cope with trauma, recover from survivalism, or engage in shadow magic.

Estha McNevin

 October 24

Saturday

2nd ♓

☽ v/c 7:18 am

Color of the day: Gray
Incense of the day: Sage

Maladay, First holyday of the Aftermath in the Discordian Calendar

If you are out of sorts today, running late, or feeling moody or clumsy, perhaps you are unwittingly celebrating Maladay, one of the holydays of the religion Discordianism. This belief system honors the goddess Discordia/Eris, known for causing the series of events that led to the siege of Troy. Try this spell to appease the goddess, today and any day discord threatens. Ground and center, and light a gold or yellow candle. Offer blessings to Eris. In a comfortable position, with eyes closed, slow your breathing and think of a happy occasion. Concentrate on that scene just long enough to feel a sense of harmony return. Extinguish the flame and go about your day. Pause every so often and send gratitude to Eris, to keep discord at bay. A golden apple is the symbol of the goddess, so be sure to eat a Golden Delicious apple with a meal or as a snack.

Emyme

October 25
Sunday

2nd ♓

☽ → ♈ 2:22 am

Color of the day: Gold
Incense of the day: Eucalyptus

Newborn Blessings

Give the gift of well wishes and blessings to a newborn child with this fun bottle spell. You will need a small bottle, some narrow strips of paper, a pen with purple ink, and shiny things to add to the bottle, such as confetti, glitter, and sequins.

Light a purple candle to work by, and then, on the strips of paper, write your good wishes and blessings for the new child. You might want to include things like "a life full of wonderful adventures," "bountiful love," or "I wish you peace and patience." Really any blessings will work here, as long as they are positive. Roll up the strips and plop them into the bottle. Add glitter, confetti, and other such additions until you are happy with how it looks. Seal the bottle with purple wax, and give it to the new parents.

Laurel Reufner

NOTES:

October 26

Monday

2nd ♈

☽ v/c 8:25 am

Color of the day: Gray
Incense of the day: Lilac

A Fellowfeel Spell

Today is Make a Difference Day. This holiday encourages people to connect with each other by doing volunteer work in their community. Activities include serving at a soup kitchen, building or rebuilding low-income housing, raking leaves for elderly neighbors, preparing community gardens for winter, doing maintenance work in parks, and so forth. This promotes compassion and empathy, what our ancestors called "fellowfeel."

For this spell, you'll need a loose puzzle piece and some juniper oil. Juniper boosts vigor and self-assurance. It also aids people who cut themselves off from community because of self-absorption or anxiety. Anoint the puzzle piece with juniper oil and say:

Neighbors and friends,

Meet at the ends.

Doing good deeds

And sowing seeds.

So let me learn

In my own turn.

Carry the charm with you as you do your volunteer work. Seek connections with the people you meet. Try to make at least three new friends.

Elizabeth Barrette

NOTES:

October 27

Tuesday

2nd ♈

☽ → ♉ 2:07 am

Full Moon 8:05 am

Color of the day: Red
Incense of the day: Cedar

Spell to Find Your Matron Goddess

The word *matron* comes from the old French and means "mother." With the full moon so near Samhain, the dark time of the year upon us, and the veil between the world so thin, now is a good time to find and connect with your matron goddess. Bring an offering of fresh flowers and incense or chocolate, and place these on your altar or the sacred earth before you as you deepen into meditation.

Open yourself to the mysteries of the darkness and the divine feminine. Ask your matron goddess to reveal herself to you. When she comes, take note of her appearance and the words she says to you. Ask her name and how you can best serve her, as well as what offerings she would like in the future. Allow her to embrace you, and know that you are safe. Know that you are home. Blessed be.

Thuri Calafia

 October 28

Wednesday

3rd ♉

☽ v/c 11:20 am

Color of the day: Topaz
Incense of the day: Bay laurel

Autumn Elixir Spell

Call upon the magic of autumn and create a special elixir to use for all your fall season magic and rituals. First, prepare boiling water, and pour over thinly sliced apples. Steep until cool or overnight. Add five drops of patchouli, ginger, orange, or pine essential oil; all these are associated with increasing magical potency, and patchouli is a traditional scent for the autumn season. Since clear quartz is often used to strengthen magic, place a clear quartz point in the water. Use this mixture to anoint tools and candles, to add to your bath, and any other time you use magic. Use all the mixture before winter solstice, for best results. Visualize the elixir being filled with the powers of the season.

Ember Grant

October 29

Thursday

3rd ♉

☽ → ♊ 2:24 am

Color of the day: Crimson
Incense of the day: Balsam

honor the Darkness

Samhain, or Hallows, is only two days away. We're approaching the final harvest of the year, the true beginning of winter. It's getting darker earlier each day. Contrary to religious and superstitious propaganda, darkness is not bad. If we didn't have shadows, we'd walk into walls and be one-dimensional, very boring people. If we read good books to attain "enlightment," we can also do good rituals to attain "endarkenment."

As you get ready for Samhain, clean your house. Now set up a dark altar with indigo candles and perhaps Cards I, XIII, and XX from your tarot deck. Buy or order glow-in-the-dark Fimo (polymer clay), and create a small glow-in-the-dark goddess, who can look a little like the Woman of Willendorf. Make her fat and healthy, and inscribe chevrons or a labyrinth on her. Attach her to a silken cord, and hang her in a window or wear her as a necklace.

Barbara Ardinger, PhD

 October 30

Friday

3rd ♊

☽ v/c 10:52 pm

Color of the day: White
Incense of the day: Yarrow

Decoration with Intent

In my tradition, each holiday is celebrated over three days, with the first day being preparation, the middle day being ritual, and the last day being clean-up. This being the day before Halloween, it is traditional to cook, set up the altar, and decorate. Decoration can be so much more than just making things look nice. The outfit/costume chosen, any extra tools on the altar, and even the face on the jack o' lantern can be used to project intent.

Among the many customs associated with Samhain/Halloween, there's a tradition of making a wish for the New Year. This wish can be projected and enhanced by aligning your clothing and decoration choices for the holiday with your wish. For example, if your wish is to fall in love, dress up as a love deity and tone down the scarier decorations. Decorate to promote the transformation you desire.

Michael Furie

October 31

Saturday

3rd ♊

☽ → ♋ 5:09 am

Color of the day: Brown
Incense of the day: Pine

Samhain – halloween

Crafting a Banishing Poppet

Merry Samhain! This ancient Pagan holiday is one of the most preserved in the modern Western calendar. To honor this sabbat, my community burns poppets to represent the banishing of our own unwanted dark sides.

Though the dark is not anything to be afraid of, everyone has habits, thoughts, and emotional experiences that they are not proud of. Samhain is the ideal time to send these things to the Underworld, never to return.

Simply stitch a black poppet (a small human-shaped dolly) out of black fabric. Leave the head open, and fill the body with autumn leaves and herbs for banishing, such as nettles, black pepper, red peppers, clove, garlic, and onion. Put scraps of paper in the doll that list all of the things you wish to banish from your life forever. Dedicate this poppet as a representation of those things in life that you wish to banish.

In a sacred ceremony, carefully burn the poppet to ashes while you focus on sending all these negativities away from your life forever. Be careful for what you wish for, and always be sure to leave offerings of food and flowers to the ancestors on Halloween.

Raven Digitalis

NOTES:

November

At November's commencement, the veil between the worlds is thin, and spirits linger close to the realm of the living. The Mayan Day of the Dead celebration continues until the seventh day of the month, when deceased loved ones and other spirits are bid farewell with a banquet. As the month progresses, the days get shorter and colder, and we take refuge in home, family, cozy blankets and clothes, candles, and the hearth. It's a time to rest after the hard work of the year's literal or metaphorical harvest, and to honor and enjoy the fruits of our labor. Midmonth, the Leonid meteor shower makes an appearance. Named after the constellation of Leo, from which they appear to emanate, the Leonid meteors herald the smolder-ing end of the sun's stay in Scorpio as well as its forthcoming fiery visit to Sagittarius. While the flashiness of the shower varies, it always adds a burst of brightness to the spirit while promoting authenticity, blunt honesty, and sociability. This month, be kind to your immune system by aligning with the rhythm of the season: be sure to stay warm, stay positive, get plenty of rest, and keep your environment ordered, attractive, and bright.

Tess Whitehurst

November 1
Sunday

3rd ♋

☽ v/c 10:35 pm

Color of the day: Orange
Incense of the day: Heliotrope

All Saints' Day –
Daylight Saving Time ends at 2:00 am

Saint Expedite for Success

In honor of today being All Saints' Day, let's do a little success working with the much-loved Saint Expedite. If you need something and you need it fast, Saint Expedite is your man! Expedite, without discrimination, helps those who petition him find speedy solutions and resolutions to their problems.

Find an image of Saint Expedite and set up a small altar to him on an available surface. Offer a candle (white, green, or red) and a glass of water before his image, and pray sincerely to him for what you need, with the promise of a gratitude offering when you receive it. When your request has been fulfilled, hold up your end of the agreement by offering Expedite white flowers and/or pound cake and whiskey.

Blake Octavian Blair

November 2
Monday

3rd ♋

☽ → ♌ 10:48 am

Color of the day: White
Incense of the day: Narcissus

Spell of Nine Knots

Now, as the veil thins and all of our gardens have been gathered in, it's time to look at what we've been holding on to that we no longer need in this darkening year. Take a section of black yarn or cording and tie into it nine knots. With each knot, think deeply of all your attachments, all those things you know you needn't be holding on to—your resentments, your worries, your fears. Focus your energies on those things that "knot you up" and bind you to pain and negativity. For the next nine nights, until the moon is new again, untie one knot each, and promise yourself you will let go of that particular energy pattern. When the spell is done, allow yourself to feel new and free again, and open to the energies of the season. Be blessed and be free.

Thuri Calafia

November 3
Tuesday

3rd ♌
4th Quarter 7:24 am
☽ v/c 8:46 pm

Color of the day: Black
Incense of the day: Ginger

Election Day (general)

A Spell for Tough Choices

The first Tuesday in November is Election Day in the United States—a day to make choices. There are times when choosing is easy, but when you have to weigh many options and consequences, it's not so simple. The Seven of Cups is all about choices.

Pull the Seven of Cups from a tarot deck whose images resonate with you. Place the card in front of you, and think of the choice you have to make—hold the decision as a question in your mind:

I must [decision you must make]. What should I choose?

See each cup as an option you have to pick from. Look into each one. What is the first answer that comes to you? Don't argue with yourself or think about it—just see the answer or message and write it down. What direction has the Seven of Cups given you?

Natalie Zaman

 ## November 4
Wednesday

4th ♌
☽ → ♍ 9:22 pm

Color of the day: Brown
Incense of the day: Lavender

Pantry Blessing

Gather all of your precious jewelry, available cash, and valuables for this fun spell that will bless your home with bounty and fertility throughout the seasons to come. Place your greatest valuables in kitchen cupboards, pantry baskets, and any freezers where you store your harvest. Stand in the center of your kitchen, and envision in your mind the location of each valuable.

Imagine a radiant glow that begins to emanate out of each valuable until the whole space around them begins to shine. Let this light pass into all of your food supply. See this radiant wealth as your own. Allow your treasures to remain tucked in your cupboards and pantry for the day. Energetically encourage them to fill your home with a sense of glowing wealth. Use this spell to ensure that the love and light of the season is fortified by the joy we feel when we share our bounty with others.

Estha McNevin

November 5
Thursday

4th ♏

Color of the day: Green
Incense of the day: Mulberry

Grounding Anxiety

If you suffer from anxiety or just have a stressful day, here is a quick meditative exercise to use to help release the anxious energy and restore your sense of calm. If the anxiety or stress is particularly high, this may need to be repeated a few times for the full effect.

Close your eyes, breathe deeply, and visualize a soothing ice-blue orb in the region of your solar plexus (the area above your belly button, in between the ribs) pulling all the anxiety from your body into the orb. See the anxiety as a gray haze floating around, and will that the orb inhales it like a vacuum. When you feel that all the anxiety has been absorbed into the orb, mentally send the orb down your arm to your strong hand and throw it far from you to release it.

Michael Furie

November 6
Friday

4th ♏

Color of the day: Purple
Incense of the day: Rose

From Mighty Oaks

If you ever need a kick in the pants to get something done, try this. You will need a symbol of an acorn (or an actual large acorn) and some rosemary oil. Before a lit red candle, anoint the acorn in three sets of three. With each anointing, say something such as *I will start my work and get it finished* or *I will get _____ finished.*

From then on out, simply set the acorn somewhere near you on your work surface and use it as a reminder to keep focused and on task. If motivation is needed for something more active than desk work, try to find an acorn charm and wear it when you need that extra kick.

Laurel Reufner

November 7

Saturday

4th ♏

☽ v/c 7:47 am

☽ → ♎ 10:14 am

Color of the day: Blue
Incense of the day: Ivy

Dumb Supper

Mayan Day of the Dead celebrations last one full week, and today is the last day, when transitioned souls are bid farewell with a banquet. Similarly, today would be a great day to practice the tradition known as a "dumb supper," a meal served and eaten in silence, to which you invite any deceased loved ones or deceased famous people with whom you would like to dine.

First, choose those in the spirit world that you would like to invite. Then set the table for you, any living guest(s) who would like to attend, and your spirit-world guest(s). If possible, serve something the spirit guest(s) enjoyed during their lifetime. If living guests are present, dish out food for each other rather than serving yourselves. Also dish out food for the spirit guests. Dine by candlelight, and be sure not to speak or make noise throughout the duration of the meal.

Tess Whitehurst

November 8
Sunday

4♍ ♎

☽ v/c 9:42 pm

Color of the day: Amber
Incense of the day: Juniper

Cook Something Bold and Pungent Day

No matter where you live and what the weather, know that this day is the celebration of Cook Something Bold and Pungent Day. For inspiration, call upon all household and food deities. Send special blessings to Annapurna, the Hindu goddess who embodies the divine aspect of nourishment. Ransack cookbooks and contact elder relatives for ideas. Create a new recipe, or add an extra kick to one of your favorite dishes. Gather the ingredients and tools, and bring forth your best kitchen witchery skills. Perhaps you may wish to make this a true learning experience for the next generation. Or invite your best friends or coven to participate. Ground and center, state intentions, honor the elements and directions, and dive in. Be sure your Kitchen Witch oversees the entire celebration. Start with an easy and basic braise or stock. Divide into several pots and experiment with spices and ingredients. Everyone leaves

with recipes and starter. Freeze any remaining. Say:

With love imbued,

I create this food.

From pot to plate,

This meal will sate.

Emyme

NOTES:

November 9
Monday

4ħ ♎

☽ → ♏ 11:02 pm

Color of the day: Gray
Incense of the day: Hyssop

Spirit Contact Spell

This ritual will help you contact a deceased loved one. Before you begin, smudge the space with white sage or wormwood. You'll also need a magic mirror, two white candles, and a small bell.

Light the candles on your altar, and between them place the magic mirror. Center yourself. Then softly say the person's name three times. Next, gently ring the bell three times. Softly ask the spirit to appear in the mirror. Wait quietly. You may feel a gentle touch or smell a scent associated with this person. When my grandmother is near, for example, I can smell the scent of jasmine. Before the spirit appears in the mirror, it may mist over. When the spirit appears, you may ask a question. Watch their movements— that's probably how they'll answer. Thank them and bid them farewell. Conclude by ringing the bell three times, then snuff out the candles.

James Kambos

November 10
Tuesday

4ħ ♎

Color of the day: Maroon
Incense of the day: Cinnamon

La Liberte et La Raison

The French Revolutionaries in the years after 1789 created goddesses that embodied their political ideals: liberté, raison, égalité. On November 10, 1793, a festival was held in Notre Dame Cathedral to honor these goddesses. A "temple of philosophy" was erected in the cathedral, and soon there were similar temples in churches throughout France.

Erect your own temple of philosophy. Sit comfortably before your altar and go into your alpha state. Visit a classical temple and ask to meet La Liberté, La Raison, and L'Egalité. When the goddesses appear, speak with them about wisdom, equality, and the ideals of true democracy.

When you return to normal consciousness, think about what you can place on your altar. The Statue of Liberty is sometimes said to be a goddess. Perhaps you can add your "I voted" sticker from the last election. What other symbols of liberty, reason, and equality can you add?

Barbara Ardinger, PhD

November 11
Wednesday

4th ♏

New Moon 12:47 pm

Color of the day: Topaz
Incense of the day: Marjoram

Veterans Day

New Moon of Remembrance

It is a new moon and it is also Veterans Day, the day we celebrate and honor those who have given their years—and sometimes their lives—to defend our country and the rights we hold sacred. In his 1919 proclamation of the day, President Woodrow Wilson asked that this day be filled with "solemn pride" in honoring these veterans, and the ebbing energy of today's new moon creates a perfect setting for this solemnity. The day is also sometimes called "Remembrance Day," and it is, indeed, a good time for remembering.

Rise early and walk your bounds, circling your property three times as you contemplate what it means to live in a free country and considering the many sacrifices that have made that possible. Lay flowers or a wreath on your altar space, and pause in "solemn pride" as you pay your respects to those veterans who have moved on to the Summerlands. If you can, visit a nearby veterans' monument or park. Walk the bounds there, too, reaching out and trying to connect with the spirits of the place. Thank them, bless them, and ask them to be at peace.

Susan Pesznecker

Notes:

November 12

Thursday

1st ♏︎

☽ v/c 9:54 am

☽ → ♐︎ 10:14 am

Color of the day: White

Incense of the day: Jasmine

Less Stress with Business Relationships

As we work in a business, we interact with many different types of people and we may find relationships strained. There can be many reasons for this, ranging from personal issues (theirs or yours) to business issues, which could include overwork, poor business, irritating customers, and product failures. The list can be extensive, or a combination of many issues.

A piece of sodalite that you charge and carry in your pocket can serve as a reminder that we all can be stressed, for whatever reason. If you keep it in your pocket, it will always be there to remind you.

Charge the piece of sodalite by rubbing some calming lavender oil on the stone and placing it in the moonlight, as a reminder that this is a reflection piece. Its presence should make you pause, take a moment to calm down, and reflect on how you affect others with your moods just as others affect you.

Boudica

 November 13

Friday

1st ♐︎

☽ v/c 10:19 pm

Color of the day: Rose

Incense of the day: Cypress

Washing Away the Evil Eye

Numerous cultures worldwide hold a belief in the "evil eye," or the covetous gaze. This gaze, whether symbolic or actual, holds the energy of this statement: "I want what you have, and I don't want you to have it."

To protect yourself from the evil eye, simply draw eyeballs on windows and doors in your house by using a dry-erase marker or something similar and washable. Be sure to draw some invisible eyeballs using your saliva. Burn incense at each location, and sprinkle your entire property with saltwater to form an invisible rampart.

Approach each window or door, and imagine each one glowing in white, with each eyeball glowing in a deep, rich blue. Recite any declarations of magickal intention at each location using a forceful and authoritative tone. Conclude by stating the following at each location:

Protective spirits, I summon thee. Protect me from the evil eye, so mote it be.

Raven Digitalis

November 14

Saturday

1st ♐

☽ → ♑ 7:21 pm

Color of the day: Brown
Incense of the day: Patchouli

Protective Spirits of the Land

Saturn's rule over this day always makes Saturday a nice day to honor the home and recharge its protections. One way to do this is by honoring and building a relationship with the spirits of your land. This can be done whether you live in an urban apartment, suburban house, or a rural country cottage.

Gather a couple small handfuls of an herb traditionally used for offering and/or protection, such as cedar, tobacco, or mint, and a bell or rattle. At each of the four corners of your property (in an apartment without a yard, use the four corners inside the home), rattle or ring to call the spirits' attention, and sprinkle a bit of the herb on the ground. After you have finished the fourth corner, proceed to the main altar in your home. Rattle/ring and place the remaining herbs in a bowl on the altar as an offering. So mote it be!

Blake Octavian Blair

 November 15

Sunday

1st ♑

Color of the day: Gold
Incense of the day: Marigold

A Spell for Self-Control

Earth is the element of stability and security. It buffers the volatility of fire, the mutability of water, and the flightiness of air. Draw on the power of earth if you often feel like you have no control over yourself. This can also help if you feel angry or nervous all the time.

Make an earth charm for self-control by placing a handful of garden soil on a 6 × 6-inch square of green cloth. Add a lace agate to promote emotional stability and relaxation. Add a nugget of frankincense for will and self-discipline. Add a pinch of motherwort for emotional health and appropriate boundaries. Then say:

Earth within and Earth below,

Teach me what I need to know.

Not so quick to flare or flow,

But like stone both strong and slow.

Tie the bundle closed with black thread. Store it where it won't get moved, such as under your bed.

Elizabeth Barrette

November 16
Monday

1st ♑

☽ v/c 3:53 pm

Color of the day: Lavender
Incense of the day: Neroli

The Power of Thank You

Have you ever received a gift or a nice gesture but forgot to follow up with a formal thank you? Often we say thanks but rarely acknowledge it formally. Begin a tradition of writing thank-you notes. Whenever the occasion arises, write a brief note—it will be appreciated. Everyone loves the thoughtfulness of a card and, magically, it keeps the positive energy flowing. Charge your cards with a warm and loving attitude before sending them. Use special ink. Charge an entire stack of stationery. Electronic thanks do save paper and money, but sometimes an actual card has more impact. Use recycled cards or make your own (even better). It only takes a minute to write a short note, but the impact is long-lasting. Chant:

Ink to paper I request,

In this gesture I invest,

Gratitude and thoughts sincere,

Send to those whom I hold dear.

Ember Grant

November 17
Tuesday

1st ♑

☽ → ♒ 2:24 am

Color of the day: White
Incense of the day: Bayberry

Family Harmony

This ritual is inspired by the Buddhist practice of "loving kindness meditation." Light a green candle on your altar, and sit comfortably. Place your hands on your heart. Close your eyes. Breathe deeply in and out of your heart. Then call a beloved family member to mind: someone whom you have nothing but positive feelings toward. Set a timer for three minutes, and picture this loved one receiving all the dearest desires of his or her heart. See this person smiling and laughing with joy. When the timer dings, repeat with a family member toward whom your feelings are more lukewarm or ambiguous. Then repeat the process with a family member with whom you have serious issues. Finally, repeat the process with yourself.

Tomorrow and in the days leading up to the holidays, you might want to repeat the entire process from the beginning, with the same family members or different ones.

Tess Whitehurst

November 18
Wednesday

1st ≈

Color of the day: Yellow
Incense of the day: Lilac

Cut the Mental Clutter

I'm a big proponent of seeking help for mental health issues when you need it. Just as I take medications for my diabetes, I also take medication for my chronic depression. However, sometimes, even with help, the clutter in your mind can get to be a bit much. At times like these, try this calming spell to banish the "noise," bringing yourself some needed calmness and clarity.

You will need a white candle, with a holder, and a low-sitting bowl of spring water. Set the candle and holder within the bowl, take a deep calming and centering breath, and light the candle. Sit and quietly watch the candle flame flicker as it burns. Watch its reflection within the water. Let the day's worries and aggravations slip away as the distressing noise within your mind starts to calm. This spell is best done at night.

Laurel Reufner

November 19
Thursday

1st ≈
2nd Quarter 1:27 am
☽ v/c 3:19 am
☽ → ♓ 7:21 am

Color of the day: Crimson
Incense of the day: Clove

Mirror the Mirror Spell

For this spell, you'll need a white candle, a small freestanding mirror, a picture of yourself, some card stock cut roughly the same size as the mirror, and other images from a magazine or drawings you make yourself. First, glue the picture of yourself to the card stock. Then make a "dream-building spell" collage by surrounding the picture with images of things and energy patterns, symbols, and words representing that which you most wish to draw into your life this season. Make a stand out of another small piece of card stock so the collage can stand freely. Place the picture on a windowsill or other place where you can also see the quarter moon, and place the mirror so that it reflects both the moon and the collage. Place the candle between them and light it, saying:

Double magic, double mirror, let the energies symbolized here work for me and improve my life, bringing my dreams and wishes to light.

Let the candle burn down overnight if possible.

Thuri Calafia

NOTES:

November 20
Friday

2nd ♓

Color of the day: Coral
Incense of the day: Alder

Let Time Stand Still

At this time of year, nature goes dormant. This spell takes a cue from nature and gives you time to pause and reflect. For this spell, you'll need a small clock, a black cloth, and your favorite soap, bubble bath, body lotion, etc.

First run a nice warm bath for yourself with your favorite soap/bubble bath. Place the clock near the tub, and cover it with the black cloth. For this spell, time means nothing. Remove your bathrobe; let it fall to the floor, and as it does, visualize all your earthly cares being removed from your shoulders. Step into the tub and sink into the water. Don't worry about the time—for once, turn your mind off!

When you're ready—and only when you feel like it—get out of the tub. As you towel off, visualize all bad karma being removed. Now face the world.

James Kambos

November 21
Saturday

2nd ♓

☽ v/c 8:23 am

☽ → ♈ 10:12 am

Color of the day: Gray
Incense of the day: Sage

Sacred Woods

In Celtic tradition, alder, birch, elm, hazel, oak, rowan (mountain ash), willow, yew, and either holly or hawthorn are often recognized as nine "sacred woods." It is from these woods that sacred fire was made and ritual bonfires kindled. We can carry this tradition into the present by using the sacred woods for our own firecraft. If you're a traditionalist, work with these nine, but if other woods speak to you with deeper meaning, you can develop your own list. Collect small pieces of each wood, and create small bundles, tied with cotton string. Use these bundles to kindle your own ritual fires. For smaller-scale altar or candle work, work with wood shavings instead. As you light the fires, chant:

Fire, fire, burning bright,
sacred woods and kindled light.

Repeat the chant until your flames are blazing.

Susan Pesznecker

November 22
Sunday

2nd ♈

☉ → ♐ 10:25 am

☽ v/c 2:16 pm

Color of the day: Yellow
Incense of the day: Frankincense

In-Between Spell

Today the sun moves from the sign of Scorpio into Sagittarius, a time of in between. The uncertainty of being neither here nor there can be uncomfortable and frustrating. As the moon waxes, do this spell to appreciate times of in between, and know the scales will tip and set you on your path again when the time is right.

Ground and center yourself, then raise your hands as if you were a human scale, your palms open to the sky, and speak this incantation:

Betwixt and between,

Neither here nor there.

Still, I am exactly where I need to be.

Feel the weight of one side and then the other go up and down, evening out. Repeat the incantation until you feel that both sides are even. Take three deep, cleansing breaths, then sweep your arms to the heavens and down to your sides, balance restored.

Natalie Zaman

November 23

Monday

2nd ♈

☽ → ♉ 11:26 am

Color of the day: White
Incense of the day: Clary sage

Aura of Protection

For a super simple protection spell, all you need is a white candle and some olive oil. Anoint the candle with the oil, light it, and visualize yourself in a mirrored egg of protection. The mirror reflects any negativity sent your way. When your mental image is strong, say:

Mirrored orb of strength and might,

Block all negativity.

Deflect darkness, let in light,

Of any harm, I am free.

Michael Furie

NOTES:

November 24
Tuesday

2nd ♉

☽ v/c 8:26 pm

Color of the day: Gray
Incense of the day: Basil

Confusion Is for the Birds

It's easy for sensitive people to get overwhelmed by life's twists and turns. Human drama can be difficult to process and can create a mental whirlpool of confusing emotions. To help separate yourself from this energy, consider performing this spell.

Visit a forested area of nature where you know wild birds are plentiful. Bring a large bag of wild birdseed. Calm your mind and enter a state of quietude in order to reflect on the "peaceful chaos" of nature. Take a series of deep breaths to invoke this energy into yourself, envisioning your mental chaos dripping down your body and into the birdseed beneath you. Direct all of this confusion into the birdseed. After a few minutes, hold your hands over the birdseed and say the following while you visualize birds consuming every seed:

Creatures of the air, great winged messengers! I give you this offering and ask that you take from me this chaos and confusion. Please digest, transmute, and transform these dark thoughts into a fertilizer for the lush future. I humbly beg your assistance!

Scatter the birdseed all around you, visualizing the birds happily absorbing this energy in order to transform it into peaceful tranquility for both themselves and you.

Raven Digitalis

NOTES:

November 25

Wednesday

2nd ♉

☽ → ♊ 12:15 pm

Full Moon 5:44 pm

Color of the day: White

Incense of the day: Honeysuckle

Full Moon Ritual

> *Whenever ye have need of anything,*
> *once in the month, and better it be*
> *when the Moon is full, then shall ye*
> *assemble in some secret place and adore*
> *the spirit of She, who is Queen of all*
> *witches.*

—Doreen Valiente, Charge of the Goddess

A full moon ritual for a solitary does not need to be fancy or complex. It is more about your connection with your Goddess and what is needed in your life at this time.

No altar is needed. Rather, just stand in the moonlight, close your eyes, and feel her presence. Talk with her about how things are with you. How is life for you right now? Is there anything that could make it better? Or is life too much, and maybe you could do better with less, like less strain or less stress? It is all about you at this moment, and your Goddess is there if you will just reach out and make the connection.

Take this evening to talk to your Goddess. Thank her for all the good

things in your life. And do not be afraid to ask her for any assistance you may need. That is what a full moon is all about.

Boudica

NOTES:

November 26

Thursday

3rd ♊

☽ v/c 10:35 pm

Color of the day: Purple
Incense of the day: Apricot

Thanksgiving Day

Giving Thanks

Everyone who's read any New Age books knows about that good old "attitude of gratitude." Let's get this ideal grounded on Thanksgiving Day.

First thing in the morning, make a list of five simple things you're grateful for in your life. (You slept well last night. Your shoes and socks are comfortable. That sort of little thing.) After you do your fair share of housecleaning and/or meal preparation, sit down again and add to your list: write five grander things for which you're grateful. (You're not homeless; you live indoors. You always have enough to eat. You have simpatico friends.) Whether you eat your Thanksgiving feast at home with your family or go somewhere for a potluck with friends, take time to tell each person why you're grateful to have him or her in your life. At bedtime, add five more things to your gratitude list. Lest you forget, keep the list on your altar.

Barbara Ardinger, PhD

 November 27

Friday

3rd ♊

☽ → ♋ 2:27 pm

Color of the day: Pink
Incense of the day: Vanilla

Buy Nothing Day

Today is the day after Thanksgiving in the United States, a day that has come to be one of the busiest and most lucrative shopping days of the year. But it can also be seen as a day of excess and greed. Instead of falling into this pattern, declare today Buy Nothing Day. Make not one purchase; merely begin planning and list making.

Starting today and over the weekend, haul out all those boxes of winter/holiday decorations, even the ones you have not opened in years. Start a discard box, a go-through-again box, and a keep box. Light a white or green candle with a holiday scent. Put holiday music or a movie on for background sound. Offer gratitude for blessings and request clear thinking. Keep up your strength; fortify yourself with a robust meal using any leftovers you froze from November 8th. Donate whatever items you discard to your local thrift store or craft co-op.

Emyme

November 28

Saturday

3rd ♋

Color of the day: Black
Incense of the day: Rue

Cleansing and Blessing the Car

For this spell, assemble:

- Two gallons distilled vinegar

- One lemon, rolled firmly and then juiced

- Eight drops pure essential tangerine oil, to brighten your path

- Eight drops pure essential holy basil oil, to bless your path

- Three drops pure essential frankincense oil, to remove all impediments

Take two cups of distilled vinegar from the gallon jug, and use it to wash the wheels of your car. Roll and juice the lemon, then add it to the distilled vinegar. Next add in the essential oils. As you do so, announce the quality you would like to evoke from each oil. Cap the jug and shake it vigorously.

Add one cup of this car cleansing and blessing potion to any two-gallon bucket of soapy water. Dilute ¼ cup in a spray bottle with one cup vodka and one cup water to make a glass and surface spray for the windows, mirrors, and interior of your vehicle. When all of your dilutions are ready, wash and bless your car inside and out, to protect you on the road.

Estha McNevin

Notes:

November 29

Sunday

3rd ♋

☽ v/c 7:46 am

☽ → ♌ 7:47 pm

Color of the day: Orange
Incense of the day: Hyacinth

Saint Andrew's Eve

In many parts of Europe, this is a night for fortunetelling—dripping hot wax into a bowl of cold water, reading tea leaves, even interpreting the shapes of shadows. Yet in some areas, like Romania, this was once considered a night of fearsome activity, when corpses could return from the grave to haunt their relatives. Use this night to practice the divination technique of your choice, or perhaps try a new one. Maybe even reach out to the spirits of your ancestors, if you desire. Chant:

Drawing from the days of old,

Fortunes that would be foretold.

Lend your power to this night,

Grant me wisdom, give me sight.

Ember Grant

 November 30

Monday

3rd ♌

Color of the day: Ivory
Incense of the day: Lily

Linga Mudra

The linga mudra activates the masculine principle and reinforces the fire element in the body. (The term *linga* is Sanskrit for phallus, the male generative organ.) This promotes sexual energy and body heat. Use this mudra to deal with chills from cold weather, to dry out wet illnesses such as colds or coughs, to ease asthma aggravated by weather changes, and to relieve male impotence. The linga mudra also alleviates the kind of depression that brings feelings of lethargy and darkness.

Sit up straight. This mudra requires both hands. Place your palms together. Interlace and close your fingers. Keep your left thumb vertically erect, like a candle flame, and encircle it with the thumb and index finger of your right hand. Concentrate on a feeling of warmth rising straight up through your body, filling you with vigor.

This mudra is better suited to use when needed for a specific complaint, rather than everyday practice.

Elizabeth Barrette

December

Decmber, in the minds of many, is both the quintessential winter month and one of the busiest months of the year. It is a month full of joyous celebrations from many traditions. Advent, Bodhi Day, Saturnalia, Kwanzaa, Pancha Ganapati, Christmas, Hanukkah, and Yule are just a small selection of festivals that have their calendrical home in the month of December.

The themes of light (literal, energetic, and metaphorical), wisdom, and goodwill are a common thread among many of the celebrations. This is a good time of year to remember that despite our differences, we have much in common with one other. In a modern culture where many of us practice religious and spiritual pluralism to some degree, December presents more than one holy festival for each of us to nurture our spirit.

In the Northern Hemisphere, the winter solstice marks the official start of winter—a season of introspection. Though the land appears outwardly to be in a quiet slumber, we know that beneath the soil, down in the roots and in the dens of animals, there is a process of incubative growth occurring. Once again, the seasons of our soul align in harmony with the seasons of nature.

Blake Octavian Blair

December 1

Tuesday

3rd ♌

☽ v/c 10:09 pm

Color of the day: Scarlet
Incense of the day: Geranium

World AIDS Day

Much of the world has come very far in the treatment of AIDS. There is a better understanding of the causes and non-contagious nature of the disease. Treatment has improved dramatically. Contracting AIDS is no longer the death sentence it used to be.

Unfortunately, ignorance and superstitions about the disease still exist. In your castings today, light a candle and say a prayer for those living with AIDS, for those countries still suffering, and for the governments and religious leaders still cloaked in ignorance.

To all the deities of all religions and belief systems in the world or to just one, say:

Send a light,
A light of health.
Send a light,
A light of hope.
Open a mind,
Open a heart.

Send a light,
Banish the dark.
Send a light,
Bring peace.

Emyme

NOTES:

December 2
Wednesday

3rd ♌
☽ → ♍ 5:09 am

Color of the day: White
Incense of the day: Marjoram

The Goddess Is in the Details

Have you ever seen a painting by Georges-Pierre Seurat? From a distance, the details are a haze of soft lines and colors, but up close, each image is made of tiny points of color, each important to the whole composition. Sometimes we forget our worth, especially at a time of the year when everything seems so commercial. On this, Seurat's birthday, take a moment to remember your vital place in the world.

Close your eyes and picture the universe—vast and filled with stars and planets. Now draw your focus closer: universe to galaxy, galaxy to planet… With each inward draw, recite or think this incantation:

I am an integral part

Of an intricate universe.

Earth… to continent… to country… to city… to street… to house… until you see yourself. Repeat the incantation whenever you need a reminder that you are wanted, needed, and loved.

Natalie Zaman

December 3
Thursday

3rd ♍
4th Quarter 2:40 am
☽ v/c 11:59 pm

Color of the day: Turquoise
Incense of the day: Nutmeg

Ease the Way

Misunderstandings happen at the best of times, but at the holidays they can be especially distressful. Use this stovetop-simmering potpourri to help ease nerves now and throughout the month.

Charge about ¼ cup each of the following herbs before adding them to a small saucepan of water: sweetgrass (blessings), lemon peel (courage), roses (love), lavender (peace), and cedar (purification). Allow the potpourri to simmer and scent your home. Replenish the herbs as the aroma starts to disappear.

Laurel Reufner

December 4

Friday

4th ♏

☽ → ♎ 5:34 pm

Color of the day: Rose
Incense of the day: Rose

Spell of Self-Care

As the winter holidays approach, it's easy to get caught up in the general grouchiness and obligation energies of the season. Try to remember the joy of true giving, and take a day to give something to yourself—a real gift! Lock your doors, turn off your phone, stay off the Internet, and breathe! Deepen into meditation, and ask your most beloved deities what your spirit most needs to replenish and recharge today. Carve and anoint a candle of blessing for yourself. Be sure to add blessings of peace and health, strength and prosperity. Take a long soak in the tub or hot shower before entering the circle. Then burn the candle, saying:

> As I light this candle, so I rekindle my
> own inner fire and drive through rest
> and peace and healing.

Then take some time to meditate on what special gift you'll be getting for yourself this Yule, and be blessed.

Thuri Calafia

 December 5

Saturday

4th ♎

Color of the day: Brown
Incense of the day: Magnolia

Holiday Spending Spell

The shopping rush is on for the holidays, and it's easy to overspend, but this spell will help with that. You'll need these items: snow or ice, a one-quart freezer bag, and a one dollar bill.

Place the dollar in the freezer bag as you think, *I'm in control.* Now pack snow or ice over the dollar as you visualize yourself putting a "freeze" on your spending. Close the bag and toss it in the freezer. When you go shopping, go with a shopping list. As you reach your spending limit, say to yourself, *Freeze it.* Keeping the spell in your mind as you shop will prevent overspending.

Keep your assets "frozen" until after Christmas. Then take the freezer bag from your freezer, let it thaw, remove the dollar, and pour the water outside.

James Kambos

December 6

Sunday

4th ♎

☽ v/c 9:03 pm

Color of the day: Amber
Incense of the day: Almond

Banish holiday Weight Gain

Today, reverse the trend of holiday weight gain. Draw a warm bath. Add:

- One cup Epsom salt
- ½ cup sea salt
- ¼ cup baking soda
- The peels from one grapefruit, one orange, and one tangerine

Stir the water in a counterclockwise direction to dissolve the salt and release the citrus essence. Light a white candle. Stand over the water, and direct your palms toward it. Close your eyes and visualize very bright white light coming out through the palms of your hands. Say:

*Goddess Venus and Spirit of Air,
I call on you! I call on your beauty,
I call on your joy. May I walk with
lightness and feel sustained by inspiration, nourishing breath, and healthy
food choices. Please fill this water with
positivity and peace. Thank you.*

Bathe for at least forty minutes, making sure to drink plenty of fresh water before and after.

Tess Whitehurst

Notes:

December 7

Monday

4th ♎

☽ → ♏ 6:26 am

Color of the day: White
Incense of the day: Neroli

hanukkah begins

The Fivefold Kiss

To give yourself a magickal boost to help you through your day, try performing a modification of the Wiccan Fivefold Kiss. Though this was originally designed to prepare a person for invocation or initiation, you can certainly use a variation of it as a self-blessing.

Get a small bottle of your favorite essential oil—please note that "fragrant" oil is chemical and should not be used for magickal work. If essential oil is unavailable, simply use olive oil or mineral oil.

Take some deep breaths and put yourself in a meditative state of mind. Anoint the tops of your feet and say:

Blessed be my feet, which have brought me in my ways.

Anoint your knees and say:

Blessed be my knees, which shall kneel before the sacred altar.

Anoint your genitals and say:

Blessed be my (womb/phallus), without which we would not be.

Anoint your chest and say:

Blessed be my chest, formed in perfect strength.

Anoint your lips and say:

Blessed be my lips, which shall utter the sacred names.

Raven Digitalis

NOTES:

December 8

Tuesday

4th ♏

Color of the day: Black
Incense of the day: Ginger

Caroling

Caroling has always been a traditional Yuliday activity—but how long has it been since you actually went caroling? Combine singing and winter ritual with a Yule caroling party. Choose carols with Pagan-style lyrics, or rewrite your own lyrics. Invite guests to gather early to work through the songs. Before leaving, circle together and ask everyone to share their holiday season wishes or intentions. Then head out to sing! As you walk and then sing, be aware of the rising energy—feel the joy and let it spill from you.

Upon returning home, circle up again, and share reflections on the caroling experience. Hold hands, sing a final quiet song together, and pause for a silent moment as the energy settles. Conclude your Yuletide ritual with cakes and ale of your choice. Happy holidays!

Susan Pesznecker

December 9
Wednesday

4th ♏

☽ v/c 1:39 am

☽ → ♐ 5:25 pm

Color of the day: Yellow
Incense of the day: Lavender

A Hero's Welcome

When problems become too large to cope with, we are left with no other option than to look for external help. Calling to an ambiguous GOD alone may not be enough. In the Old World, our Pagan myths were designed to give us guidance and support whenever we heard them retold. Even today, we can turn to the comfort of our oral traditions.

Welcoming a hero into your life is symbolic of being granted help that is much needed, and earnestly asked for. Today, discover the type of heroic energy missing in your life by employing traditional hero-gods from a timeless epic of Western culture, Homer's *Iliad*.

Write out or print the mythic stories for Hercules, Achilles, Odysseus, David, and Aries/Mars. Use thick fancy parchment paper. Be sure to include images of them, information about the weapons they were skilled at using, and the overarching moral of their character.

Roll up each parchment, affix a red wax seal, and bind the scroll in rust-colored ribbon. Place all five into a hat that you wear.

Like all quests for insight, salvation, or redemption, a wondrous act must be performed for the answer you seek to be revealed. Complete one very large act of kindness today. At the end of the day, draw the hero who is most needed in your life from your hat. Apply his myth to your own life by learning to master the skills, morals, and themes of our ancient Pagan heroes.

Estha McNevin

NOTES:

December 10
Thursday

4th ♐

Color of the day: Purple
Incense of the day: Myrhh

Increase Your Money

At this time of year, we could all use some extra cash. Keep a piece of malachite in your purse to ensure you will never be broke. A piece of peridot in your pocket will do the same. A silver coin is also a good talisman to keep so you will never be without cash.

A piece of devil's shoestring (honeysuckle) in your pocket at a job interview helps to increase your chances of landing that job. It is also good to keep in your pocket when you ask for that raise at work!

Burning patchouli during a money spell adds abundance. Set a piece of bryony (*Bryonia alba*) root on your money to increase prosperity. Burn chamomile or add some to your spell bag to increase money. Sprinkle Irish moss in your wallet for gaining and keeping a steady income of money.

Boudica

December 11
Friday

4th ♐
New Moon 5:29 am
☽ v/c 11:06 am

Color of the day: Pink
Incense of the day: Mint

New Moon of Waning Fire

This new moon (in Sagittarius) can be used to gather up solar energy to be used for things like travel magic or to ward off seasonal affective disorder. For this, you will need one length of red cord and two lengths of black cord (twelve to eighteen inches long, each), a red candle and an orange candle, and black clothing.

Place the red candle on the left of the altar and the orange candle on the right. Light the candles, and begin to braid the cords together. Tie a knot at the top, and braid down to the bottom. Tie another knot in the bottom and then six more knots in the cord. As you tie each knot, visualize and ask that the light and warmth of the sun be held within each knot. Once the cord is complete, you can wear or carry it to help you through fall and winter.

Michael Furie

December 12

Saturday

1st ♐

☽ → ♑ 1:46 am

Color of the day: Gray
Incense of the day: Sandalwood

How Will Your Garden Grow?

Deepest, darkest winter seems like a strange time for gardening, but the cold days of winter, when the ground is hard and plants are hibernating, are a good time to get out your gardening and plant books and plan your spring garden.

First, visualize your garden-to-be. Is it filled with veggies? Herbs? Flowers? A combination? Will you be gardening at home or in a public space? If you decide to make any changes, make notes. Do you need to start composting? Buy seeds or baby plants? Stakes and string? Consider the magical aspects of a garden, such as its shape, what plants are friendly with each other, flowers that attract bees and butterflies, and magical herbs you'll need during the year. Be sure to find statues of the Green Man and at least one garden goddess—start with Xochiquetzel, Ceres, or Demeter—to place in your garden.

Barbara Ardinger, PhD

 December 13

Sunday

1st ♑

☽ v/c 6:07 pm

Color of the day: Yellow
Incense of the day: Marigold

Saint Lucy's Day Votive Candle Offering

The actual Saint Lucy was Italian, but she was adopted as part of the Swedish winter solstice customs. She is depicted in a white gown, crowned with glowing candles and bearing sweets and coffee or mulled wine. Bake sweet treats today and make a votive offering of light.

Light a candle for something meaningful to you, and sit for a while in peaceful meditation. Give thanks, say a prayer for a loved one, ask for guidance or whatever you need—but it should be sincere. Sit or kneel in front of the candle for a moment and meditate; focus your intent. Put the candle in a window or in another safe but visible location so you are reminded of it. Make this candle special. Use a votive holder that you save for special occasions, or buy a candle of an unusual color. If you make candles, pour a special one for today.

Ember Grant

December 14

Monday

1st ♑

☽ → ♒ 7:59 am

Color of the day: Gray
Incense of the day: Hyssop

hanukkah ends

A Candle Storage Blessing

This is the end of Hanukkah. This holiday celebrates the struggle for religious freedom, something many Pagans can relate to. After nightfall, and following Shabbat, Jewish families recite blessings, light eight candles in the menorah, and recite Havdalah.

Now is a good time to think about how you store your candles intended for magical and spiritual purposes. The best container for them is a wooden box, such as a cigar box. Paint, carve, or otherwise decorate your box with symbols of protection and fire, like a pentagram or dragon's eye. Whenever you put away your candles, trace a pentagram over the lid of the box with your finger. Then say:

Creatures of fire, now sleep tight

Until I have need of your light.

Keep the box of candles in a cool, dark place. Don't store them in the refrigerator or freezer. A closet is usually ideal.

Elizabeth Barrette

December 15

Tuesday

1st ♒

Color of the day: Red
Incense of the day: Cedar

Winter Health Protection Tonic

Even the most diligent winter anti-illness regimen can use a little fortification. Done in the first waxing moon period of the season (good energy for building), this spell will help protect against the flu and the winter blues.

Fill a clean spray bottle with water. Add three pinches of salt for purity and protection, and three small appropriate stones. Amber is a wonderful stone for vitality and warmth, but others, such as jade for general good health or black tourmaline for protection (or a combination of all three), will work too. Adding a quartz crystal will magnify the qualities of any other stones you choose.

Working clockwise around your home, spray the corner of each room, as well as the windows and doors, speaking the following incantation:

Strength and health,

Comfort and joy,

For all who enter here.

So mote it be!

Repeat to recharge the energy throughout the season.

Natalie Zaman

 December 16

Wednesday

1st ♒

☽ v/c 2:17 am

☽ → ♓ 12:45 pm

Color of the day: Brown
Incense of the day: Honeysuckle

Touchstone for Decisiveness

Is there a decision you need to make that is gnawing away at you? Aventurine, a stone whose energies resonate well with Wednesday, is just the ticket to assist in boosting decisiveness. This stone also helps stabilize the mind and assists with leadership.

Simply take a small piece of aventurine and hold it to your heart (its associated chakra). Think of the decision you need to make, and recite the following incantation:

Stone of the heart and decisive mind,

Clear perception and perseverance shall be mine.

For with calm and clarity, a decision I shall find.

So mote it be!

Carry the stone with you in a pocket or in a bag on a cord around your neck. Keep the stone on your person until you feel comfortable and confident that you have arrived at a definite decision about your situation.

Blake Octavian Blair

December 17

Thursday

1st ♈ ♓

Color of the day: White
Incense of the day: Mulberry

Saturnalia Begins

Today marks the beginning of the Roman celebration of Saturnalia, one of the roots of the Christmas celebration. This festival lasted about a week and was intended to honor the god Saturn and included giving gifts and general merry making, in addition to role reversal. To kick off your season of holiday celebrations, make Saturnalia gifts for your friends and family members.

In many cultures, boughs of evergreen represent everlasting life. Create mini boughs of pine, cedar, and holly to hang in the home. Tie them together with red ribbon, and decorate them as you choose. Attach a tag with the following message to each one you give away, offering blessings for the season:

Blessings for your home and hearth,

Joyful times of love and warmth.

Family and friends be near,

Wishing you delight and cheer.

Ember Grant

NOTES:

December 18

Friday

1st ♈ ♓

☽ v/c 10:14 am

2nd Quarter 10:14 am

☽ → ♈ 4:26 pm

Color of the day: Purple
Incense of the day: Yarrow

Filled with Love and Light

For this spell, assemble:

- 777 small beeswax candles, for the goddess Venus (yes, 777!)
- One fluid ounce essential rose oil in jojoba
- ¼ cup raw honey
- One cup honey mead

Sit in a central location of your home. Anoint the wick of a candle with honey. As you do so, say:

Bees that bumble, bustle, and buzz, beget the nectar of the Gods Divine.

Next, massage rose oil into the wax, and call flirtatiously to Venus:

Lady blessed, of love's design, unfold your flower of light throughout space and time.

Charge each candle with your own feelings of universal love. This spell will only yield its results if you take the time to bless each candle individually and then light it immediately; place it somewhere safely in the room.

Take a moment to envision the light of the flame penetrating the very essence of your cellular and spiritual bodies simultaneously, as it illuminates everything around you. As you finish one candle, move quickly on to the next.

When all the candles are lit, express your prayers to the goddess of all love and light clearly and concisely. (Be sure to take any necessary safety precautions when lighting so many candles.) Soak up the divine light of the creating mother of the universe. Allow the radiant beauty of the goddess to fill your being.

When you are ready, snuff out the candles by pinching the wick between two fingers wetted with honey mead. Then give away each and every candle throughout the day as an act of devotion to the goddess of selfless love.

Estha McNevin

Notes:

December 19
Saturday

2nd ♈

Color of the day: Black
Incense of the day: Sage

Spell for Capturing Warmth

Since it is very late fall and almost winter, a spell designed to help us retain warmth may be helpful. To cast this spell, gather a red candle and cinnamon oil. Anoint the candle with the oil, and charge the candle to hold the power of the sun. Ask for the power of the sun to shine down and be directed into the candle. Now, light the candle and visualize that as the candle burns, it transfers the warmth from the flame into your solar plexus, located about three inches above your belly button. Say:

Flame of candle, renew inner fire,

Keep me warm despite the chill.

Comforting heat is my desire,

Feel of summer is what I will.

Allow the candle to burn as long as you can, envisioning your solar plexus building up a reserve of warmth to sustain you throughout the cold half of the year. Extinguish the candle.

Michael Furie

December 20
Sunday

2nd ♈

☽ v/c 5:01 pm
☽ → ♉ 7:13 pm

Color of the day: Gold
Incense of the day: Juniper

Time to Remember Spell

Deep in December, it's time to remember those we've lost touch with, or those who are no longer on this earth. As the hustle and bustle of the holidays reaches its peak, here is a spell to help you connect.

Cover your altar in red fabric, and place two bayberry-scented candles on it. If you wish, add photos. Think of someone you wish to contact. Envision their face in your mind. As you think of them, light the candles and move them close together. If you're thinking of someone deceased, send loving thoughts their way. Then whisper:

In December when the world is aglow,

It's time to remember

The loved ones it's nice to know.

While the candles burn, write a note to at least one person you've thought of. In this way, you're creating a chain of good karma. Be alert for any psychic messages coming to you, and mail the note.

James Kambos

December 21

Monday

2nd ☿

☉ → ♑ 11:48 pm

Color of the day: Silver
Incense of the day: Narcissus

Yule – Winter Solstice

Yule Sabbat Spell

Arise this Yule before anyone else in your household, and watch the sun come up. As the dawn ascends on this day, ponder newness, fresh ideas, change. If you have a drum, allow yourself to tune in to the Mother's heartbeat as the Son rises, and drum him awake! You can also sing him up with any number of holiday carols. If you listen closely, you'll hear the Old Religion coming through in the guise of the New one. Open your heart to the joy of the earth as the new Sun God is born. Allow his light and energy to fill your entire being: heart, mind, emotions, passions, spirit, body. Dance with the energy, and know that today, you have carte blanche to start your life anew. Take a piece of paper and jot down any inspirations you have at this time, and place the paper on your altar where you'll see it as the Wheel continues to turn. Be blessed, knowing that you have the power to change your life!

Thuri Calafia

 December 22

Tuesday

2nd ☿

☽ v/c 9:26 am

☽ → ♊ 9:31 pm

Color of the day: White
Incense of the day: Basil

Buche de Noel

Today, bake a Yule log cake, or *buche de Noel*, to warm hearts, sweeten moods, and honor the Yuletide spirit. (To go easy on the earth and your health, find a vegan recipe or substitute with vegan margarine, egg substitute, and soymilk. You can also use organic sugar instead of white.) Light a red candle as you prepare it to call bright positivity into the cake. Light red and green candles on the table as you serve with coffee or tea. Before serving, say:

Today, we honor the return of brightness and the rebirth of the sun. May our hearts burn bright and golden. May we share our love and light with each other and the world. May our happiness, joy, and compassion fill this home, our community, and our world. Thank you.

Instruct your guests to keep the conversation positive and to engage in hearty laughter whenever possible.

Tess Whitehurst

December 23

Wednesday

2nd ♊

Color of the day: Topaz
Incense of the day: Lilac

Sadie, the Bargain Shopping Goddess

Do you have all your gifts ready for the holiday season? Did you already give away the best and now remember a special someone whom you really want to treat exceptionally well, and are running low on funds?

Look for Sadie, the Bargain Shopping Goddess, at the stores. Many stores start to reduce pricing on gifts close to the end of the holiday shopping season, and she will lead you to the bins with the best buys.

Who is Sadie? She is that silver-haired little old lady with a purple scarf and a gray wool coat, and she carries a big purse and lots of shopping bags. You will find her roaming the stores, running from bin to bin and shelf to shelf looking for that perfect gift.

Watch where she stops and rummages about. That shelf has exactly what you are looking for at a price you can afford.

Boudica

December 24

Thursday

2nd ♊

☽ v/c 3:04 pm

Color of the day: Green
Incense of the day: Clove

Christmas Eve

Celtic Tree Month of Birch and More

There are a number of events attributed to this day. Other than international Christmas Eve, it is Eggnog Day and National Chocolate Day. Tomorrow is the full moon, and today is the first day of the Celtic tree month of Birch. As befits this week before we celebrate secular New Year, the Birch Moon is considered a time of rebirth. The winter solstice has passed, and every day brings us just a little closer to the light of Imbolc. Over the next four weeks, any spells cast for creativity and new endeavors will have extra power. Should you be fortunate enough to have a birch tree in your yard, ward off any negative energy by tying red ribbons around the trunk or on branches.

In numerology, 12/24/2015 totals down to 8—a number connected to the planet Mercury. Remain open for divine communication. A sideways eight is the symbol of infinity.

Eggnog, chocolate, Christmas Eve, Birch Month, Mercury…today is brimming over with magical and mystical power. Cast accordingly.

Emyme

NOTES:

December 25

Friday

2nd ♊

☽ → ♋ 12:27 am

Full Moon 6:12 am

Color of the day: White
Incense of the day: Vanilla

Christmas Day

Enough Is Plenty

The full moon brings the peak of power and abundance. Christmas Day is likewise a time of giving and receiving. Let go of the idea that "more is better." It's unsustainable. Instead, embrace the principle that "enough is plenty." Want what you have.

Take time to appreciate the experience of sufficiency. Look at the pile of presents before they're unwrapped, and admire the pretty paper and ribbons. Look again after everything has been opened, and enjoy the new clothes and games and other goodies. See how happy people are. Savor the Christmas feast spread over the table. Give thanks.

Save a few tidbits—a piece of wrapping paper, some ribbon, maybe a bit of tinsel from the tree—and wrap your memories up in that, tying it off with the ribbon. Keep this as a reminder, when hard times come, that you know what it's like to have enough.

Elizabeth Barrette

 # December 26

Saturday

3rd ♋

☽ v/c 10:36 pm

Color of the day: Indigo
Incense of the day: Pine

Kwanzaa begins

Old-Fashioned Horse(shoe) Sense

Use a bit of folklore to start the coming year with not only a bit of luck, but some home protection as well.

You'll need an iron horseshoe for this spell. Check out thrift and vintage shops to try to locate one. If all else fails, get a horseshoe made for use in the game. (It probably won't have any of the holes used to hammer the shoe to the horse, so you may need to get creative when hanging it up.)

Since it's the holiday season, dress the shoe with either clove or peppermint oil, charging it with protective energies for your home. Finish with a bit of red ribbon as a bow, and hang somewhere appropriate—usually near the door. Remember to hang it ends-up so the luck doesn't run out.

Laurel Reufner

December 27

Sunday

3rd ♋

☽ → ♌ 5:31 am

Color of the day: Orange
Incense of the day: Frankincense

Journal Magick Through Space and Time

It's essential for magickal people to keep a journal of their practices, or otherwise keep a log of their spiritual activity and perceptions. Some Witches utilize a personal Book of Shadows or magickal journal. Others simply use one single book that serves as both a personal journal and a mystical journal. In either case, this spell can help provide a boost during a time of need.

Everyone goes through emotional cycles. Sometimes we need a boost of optimism and love. If you're feeling particularly low on energy, whether now or at another point in time, you may consider writing in your journal. Write about the negative emotions you're experiencing as well as something along the lines of this:

I ask my future self to send a boost of energy back through time, to me, NOW!

To make this type of magick successful, you must be willing not only to reread your journal over the years, but to focus a strong amount of healing energy to your "past self" whenever you read those words. In the present moment, if you're feeling down and choose to write those words in your journal, you should feel an immediate boost of energy from yourself in the future.

Raven Digitalis

NOTES:

December 28

Monday

3rd ♌

Color of the day: Lavender
Incense of the day: Rosemary

The Art of Rest

Chances are you've just survived some sort of holiday season, and you're tired. Let's be honest: you're exhausted. It's time for some intentional R&R.

Clear two or three evening hours, and arrange a favorite meal that requires little or no preparation. Begin with a silent walk: no electronics and no iPod, please—just you and the world in silent communion. Be aware of your feet touching the ground with each step, of the sights and sounds around you, of the air moving in and out of your lungs.

When you arrive home, drink a glass of cool water, and visualize it nurturing every cell in your body. Enjoy your dinner, then slip into a hot bath scented with lavender oil or salts. Dry with a soft towel, slip on clean PJs, and relax with a good book, repeating:

After the day,

Cares slip away.

Quiet blessings o'er me,

The world blessed be.

Susan Pesznecker

December 29

Tuesday

3rd ♌

☽ v/c 12:38 pm

☽ → ♍ 1:58 pm

Color of the day: Black
Incense of the day: Cinnamon

Take Back Control

Sometimes we find that our lives, or parts of our lives, may have gotten way past our ability to deal with them. In these cases, we need to resolve the issue by bringing it under control. You know when it happens—when you finally realize that you're not happy with the way things currently are and you know they could be better if only you could stop _____.

It may be money or people in your life that are straining your other relationships. First you need to pinpoint the source of the problem. Is it job-related or is it someone in your life? Do some scrying with a mirror or candle, and look deep at the situation that is making your life difficult. Once that is determined, set up a plan to deal with it.

Ask your gods or your HGA or your higher self to help you overcome your difficulties. Start now! The sooner you get to working on those out-of-control issues, the sooner you can get back on track to what you want your life to be.

Boudica

December 30

Wednesday

3rd ♍

Color of the day: White
Incense of the day: Bay laurel

Numerology

Today has occasionally been considered an intercalary day, meaning it's at the end of the year and doesn't really count. We can make it count and find its meaning with numerology. Use the meanings of numbers given below, and find a good book or website to augment them. Do the math:

December =
D + E + C + E + M + B + E + R =
4 + 5 + 3 + 5 + 4 + 2 + 5 + 9 =
37 = 3 + 7 = 10 = 1

As the first digit, 1 means creation, individuation, self-assertion, self-reliance.

December 30 = 1 + 3 = 4

Some people think 4 just means hard work, but it also means endurance, reliance on facts, success, and creativity.

December 30, 2015 =
1 + 3 + 2 + 1 + 5 = 12 = 1 + 2 = 3

And 3 means personal expression, adornment, and the arts.

It looks like today is a good day to assert yourself, be creative but stay grounded, and dress up and go to a year-end party. Hooray!

By the way, 2016 = 9

The last digit, 9, means complete expression, intuition, deeper understanding, and philanthropy. Next year may be the end of a cycle in your life. Stay tuned!

Barbara Ardinger, PhD

Notes:

December 31
Thursday

3rd ♍

Color of the day: Crimson
Incense of the day: Carnation

New Year's Eve

New Year's Eve Spiritual Spritz

Many Peruvian people take part in a New Year's Eve tradition that entails visiting a shaman to have a technique called spritzing performed on them. Spritzing entails the spraying, from a shaman's mouth, of a sacred infusion or holy water for various purposes, including honoring spirits, cleansing, protection, healing, or removing heavy or detrimental energies. On New Year's Eve, the shaman traditionally uses a chamomile infusion to spritz the person, with the intention of warding off evil spirits in the new year.

To spritz the traditional way, while extremely effective, takes great practice. But have no fear, you can use a spray bottle! Simply steep a few chamomile tea bags in boiling water and let the infusion cool to room temperature. Fill your bottle with it, and spritz yourself, or exchange spritzes with a loved one, to assist in warding off less admirable energies and entities in the coming year.

Blake Octavian Blair

NOTES:

Daily Magical Influences

Each day is ruled by a planet that possesses specific magical influences:

Monday (Moon): peace, healing, caring, psychic awareness, purification.

Tuesday (Mars): passion, sex, courage, aggression, protection.

Wednesday (Mercury): conscious mind, study, travel, divination, wisdom.

Thursday (Jupiter): expansion, money, prosperity, generosity.

Friday (Venus): love, friendship, reconciliation, beauty.

Saturday (Saturn): longevity, exorcism, endings, homes, houses.

Sunday (Sun): healing, spirituality, success, strength, protection.

Lunar Phases

The lunar phase is important in determining best times for magic.

The waxing moon (from the new moon to the full moon) is the ideal time for magic to draw things toward you.

The full moon is the time of greatest power.

The waning moon (from the full moon to the new moon) is a time for study, meditation, and little magical work (except magic designed to banish harmful energies).

Astrological Symbols

The Sun	☉	Aries	♈
The Moon	☽	Taurus	♉
Mercury	☿	Gemini	♊
Venus	♀	Cancer	♋
Mars	♂	Leo	♌
Jupiter	♃	Virgo	♍
Saturn	♄	Libra	♎
Uranus	♅	Scorpio	♏
Neptune	♆	Sagittarius	♐
Pluto	♇	Capricorn	♑
		Aquarius	♒
		Pisces	♓

The Moon's Sign

The moon's sign is a traditional consideration for astrologers. The moon continuously moves through each sign in the zodiac, from Aries to Pisces. The moon influences the sign it inhabits, creating different energies that affect our daily lives.

Aries: Good for starting things but lacks staying power. Things occur rapidly but quickly pass. People tend to be argumentative and assertive.

Taurus: Things begun now do last, tend to increase in value, and become hard to alter. Brings out an appreciation for beauty and sensory experience.

Gemini: Things begun now are easily changed by outside influence. Time for shortcuts, communications, games, and fun.

Cancer: Stimulates emotional rapport between people. Pinpoints need, supports growth and nurturance. Tend to domestic concerns.

Leo: Draws emphasis to the self, to central ideas or institutions, away from connections with others and emotional needs. People tend to be melodramatic.

Virgo: Favors accomplishment of details and commands from higher up. Focus on health, hygiene, and daily schedules.

Libra: Favors cooperation, compromise, social activities, beautification of surroundings, balance, and partnership.

Scorpio: Increases awareness of psychic power. Favors activities requiring intensity and focus. People tend to brood and become secretive under this moon sign.

Sagittarius: Encourages flights of imagination and confidence. This moon sign is adventurous, philosophical, and athletic. Favors expansion and growth.

Capricorn: Develops strong structure. Focus on traditions, responsibilities, and obligations. A good time to set boundaries and rules.

Aquarius: Rebellious energy. Time to break habits and make abrupt change. Personal freedom and individuality are the focus.

Pisces: The focus is on dreaming, nostalgia, intuition, and psychic impressions. A good time for spiritual or philanthropic activities.

Glossary of Magical Terms

Altar: A table that holds magical tools as a focus for spell workings.

Athame: A ritual knife used to direct personal power during workings or to symbolically draw diagrams in a spell. It is rarely, if ever, used for actual physical cutting.

Aura: An invisible energy field surrounding a person. The aura can change color depending on the state of the individual.

Balefire: A fire lit for magical purposes, usually outdoors.

Casting a circle: The process of drawing a circle around oneself to seal out unfriendly influences and raise magical power. It is the first step in a spell.

Censer: An incense burner. Traditionally a censer is a metal container, filled with incense, that is swung on the end of a chain.

Censing: The process of burning incense to spiritually cleanse an object.

Centering yourself: To prepare for a magical rite by calming and centering all of your personal energy.

Chakra: One of the seven centers of spiritual energy in the human body, according to the philosophy of yoga.

Charging: To infuse an object with magical power.

Circle of protection: A circle cast to protect oneself from unfriendly influences.

Crystals: Quartz or other stones that store cleansing or protective energies.

Deosil: Clockwise movement, symbolic of life and positive energies.

Deva: A divine being according to Hindu beliefs; a devil or evil spirit according to Zoroastrianism.

Direct/retrograde: Refers to the motion of a planet when seen from the earth. A planet is "direct" when it appears to be moving forward from the point of view of a person on the earth. It is "retrograde" when it appears to be moving backward.

Dowsing: To use a divining rod to search for a thing, usually water or minerals.

Dowsing pendulum: A long cord with a coin or gem at one end. The pattern of its swing is used to answer questions.

Dryad: A tree spirit or forest guardian.

Fey: An archaic term for a magical spirit or a fairylike being.

Gris-gris: A small bag containing charms, herbs, stones, and other items to draw energy, luck, love, or prosperity to the wearer.

Mantra: A sacred chant used in Hindu tradition to embody the divinity invoked; it is said to possess deep magical power.

Needfire: A ceremonial fire kindled at dawn on major Wiccan holidays. It was traditionally used to light all other household fires.

Pentagram: A symbolically protective five-pointed star with one point upward.

Power hand: The dominant hand; the hand used most often.

Scry: To predict the future by gazing at or into an object such as a crystal ball or pool of water.

Second sight: The psychic power or ability to foresee the future.

Sigil: A personal seal or symbol.

Smudge/smudge stick: To spiritually cleanse an object by waving smoke over and around it. A smudge stick is a bundle of several incense sticks.

Wand: A stick or rod used for casting circles and as a focus for magical power.

Widdershins: Counterclockwise movement, symbolic of negative magical purposes, sometimes used to disperse negative energies.

Spell Notes

Llewellyn's 2015 Witches' Offerings!

Packed with an astounding array of content, it's no wonder *Llewellyn's Witches' Calendar* is the top-selling calendar of its kind. It includes articles, astrological data, daily correspondences, and original full-color artwork by Kathleen Edwards.

Llewellyn's Witches' Datebook is perfect for the Witch on the go. Much more than an appointment book and calendar, this multipurpose datebook allows you to blend the magical and the mundane while keeping pace with the ever-turning Wheel of the Year. Find seasonal spells, moon rituals, sabbat recipes, astrological information, and articles, all punctuated by Edwards' inspiring artwork.

GET MORE AT LLEWELLYN.COM

Visit us online to browse hundreds of our books and decks, plus sign up to receive our e-newsletters and exclusive online offers.

- Free tarot readings • Spell-A-Day • Moon phases
- Recipes, spells, and tips • Blogs • Encyclopedia
- Author interviews, articles, and upcoming events

GET SOCIAL WITH LLEWELLYN

Find us on Facebook

www.Facebook.com/LlewellynBooks

Follow us on

www.Twitter.com/Llewellynbooks

GET BOOKS AT LLEWELLYN

LLEWELLYN ORDERING INFORMATION

Order online: Visit our website at www.llewellyn.com to select your books and place an order on our secure server.

Order by phone:
- Call toll free within the U.S. at 1-877-NEW-WRLD (1-877-639-9753)
- Call toll free within Canada at 1-866-NEW-WRLD (1-866-639-9753)
- We accept VISA, MasterCard, and American Express

Order by mail:
Send the full price of your order (MN residents add 6.875% sales tax) in U.S. funds, plus postage and handling to: Llewellyn Worldwide, 2143 Wooddale Drive Woodbury, MN 55125-2989

POSTAGE AND HANDLING
STANDARD (U.S. & Canada):
(Please allow 12 business days)
$25.00 and under, add $4.00.
$25.01 and over, FREE SHIPPING.

INTERNATIONAL ORDERS (airmail only):
$16.00 for one book, plus $3.00 for each additional book.

Visit us online for more shipping options. Prices subject to change.

FREE CATALOG!

To order, call
1-877-
NEW-WRLD
ext. 8236
or visit our
website